We Are Not Numbers

We Are Not Numbers
The Voices of Gaza's Youth

AHMED ALNAOUQ AND
PAM BAILEY

OLIVE
BRANCH
PRESS

An imprint of Interlink Publishing Group, Inc.
www.interlinkbooks.com

First published in 2025 by

OLIVE BRANCH PRESS
An imprint of Interlink Publishing Group, Inc.
46 Crosby Street, Northampton, Massachusetts 01060
www.interlinkbooks.com

This selection copyright © Ahmed Alnaouq and Pam Bailey, 2025

Text copyright © Haneen AbdAlnabi, Neda Abadla, Ismail Abu-Aitah, Haya Abu Shammala, Mosab Abu Toha, Lubna Abuhashem, Hanan Abukmail, Akram Abunahla, Abdallah Abusamra, Samah Abushaibah, Ali Abusheikh, Issam Adwan, Haya Abdullah Ahmed, Hassan Alalami, Eman Alhaj Ali, Basma Almaza, Ahmed Alnaouq, Mahmoud Alnaouq, Aya Alghazzawi, Khaled Alostath, Ahmed Alsammak, Manar Alsheikh, Said Alyacoubi, Mahmoud Alyazji, Pam Bailey, Dana Besaiso, Ahmed Dader, Basman Derawi, Yusuf El-Mbayed, Maram Faraj, Enas Ghannam, Omnia Ghassan, Nada Hammad, Tala Herzallah, Hamza Ibrahim, Iman Inshasi, Anas Jnena, Yara Jouda, Hind Khoudary, Alaa Mahdi Kudaih, Yousef Maher Dawas, Malak Mattar, Roaa Missmeh, Israa Mohammed Jamal, Aya Nashwan, Butien Riman, Haneen Sabbah, Raed Sadi, Shahd Safi, Zahra Shaikhah, Eman Shawwa, Orjwan Shurrab, Reem Sleem, Huda Skaik, Asmaa Tayeh, Wejdan Wajdy Abu Shammala, Aya Zaqout, Allam Zedan, Aseel Zeineddin, Salsabeel Zeineddin, 2025

Published simultaneously in the United Kingdom by Hutchinson Heinemann, part of the Penguin Random House UK

All rights reserved. No part of this book may be reproduced in any form or by any electronic or mechanical means, including information storage and retrieval systems, without permission in writing from the publisher, except by a reviewer who may quote brief passages in a review.

Library of Congress Cataloging-in-Publication Data available
ISBN-13: 978-1-62371-581-6

Typeset in 13.5/16 pt Garamond MT Std by Jouve (UK), Milton Keynes

Printed and bound in Great Britain by Clays Ltd, Elcograf S.p.A.

10 9 8 7 6 5 4 3 2 1

Interlink Publishing is committed to a sustainable future
for our business, our readers, and our planet. This book is
made from Forest Stewardship Council® certified paper.

This anthology is dedicated to Refaat Alareer, the teacher, author, mentor and friend who guided so many of Gaza's students and future leaders (including most of our writers). His body was killed on 6 December 2023 by an Israeli air strike, but his spirit lives on.

We equally want to honour our writers who were killed in the Israeli genocide up to 9 November 2024, when this book was being edited:
Yousef Dawas, killed 14 October 2023
Mahmoud Alnaouq, killed 22 October 2023
Huda Alsoso, killed 23 October 2023
Mohammed Hamo, killed 24 November 2023

Contents

Introduction: the 'birth' of We Are Not Numbers
   by *Ahmed Alnaouq and Pam Bailey*   1

CHAPTER ONE
2015

Ayman: to the world a number; to me, my brother
   and best friend *by Ahmed Alnaouq*   13

An ode to my roof, the thin line between
   life and death *by Haya Abu Shammala*   18

A chance encounter with my teacher – and
   a tree *by Allam Zedan*   21

What makes life worth living? *by Anas Jnena*   24

An explosion of a different kind: Gaza in
   colour *by Nada Hammad*   28

A flower grows from wreckage
   by Ismail Abu-Aitah   32

A book lover's simple dream *by Khaled Alostath*   38

Friends for ever . . . we thought
   by Mosab Abu Toha   42

CHAPTER TWO
2016

Nightmare *by Malak Mattar*	49
Always on the inside looking out *by Enas Ghannam*	51
The occupation of the mind *by Aya Nashwan*	55
I am a girl *by Yara Jouda*	59
Prison is personal for Palestinians *by Salsabeel Zeineddin*	62
Mahmoud: a victim of bureaucracy, not war *by Said Alyacoubi*	66
My life is dedicated to my dad *by Hind Khoudary*	69
Love letter to Gaza *by Nada Hammad*	73

CHAPTER THREE
2017

Gazapore *by Omnia Ghassan*	81
I want the world to know *by Anas Jnena*	84
Why jello doesn't taste good any more *by Ahmed Alnaouq*	86
A sweet spot in Gaza *by Khaled Alostath*	90
English in context *by Haya Abdullah Ahmed*	95
The betrayal of Wonder Woman *by Omnia Ghassan*	99

CHAPTER FOUR
2018

How much should we risk for freedom? *by Haneen Sabbah*	105
When the sea becomes a lake: the prison that is Gaza *by Ali Abusheikh*	107
New girl on the block *by Iman Inshasi*	111
A martyr for ever, caught on camera *by Haneen AbdAlnabi*	117
A journalist grows up *by Manar Alsheikh*	121
My day of reckoning at the Great Return March *by Zahra Shaikhah*	126
Ramadan in Gaza is different this year *by Orjwan Shurrab*	131
The cost of protest *by Mahmoud Alnaouq*	135
Gazans send kites over the border *by Ahmed Alnaouq*	139

CHAPTER FIVE
2019

The world is my room *by Basman Derawi*	145
Reaching for the stars *by Abdallah Abusamra*	147
The gift of shared suffering *by Neda Abadla*	152
My battlefield is my brain *by Iman Inshasi*	156

A senseless death in Turkey *by Issam Adwan*   159
Jehad Shehada: a 'renaissance man' *by Raed Sadi*   163
Hunger 2.0: an essay on my body
   by Omnia Ghassan   167

CHAPTER SIX
2020

How does it feel? *by Yara Jouda*   177
Has the pandemic made the world like
   Gaza? *by Aya Alghazzawi*   179
One girl's joust with depression *by Asmaa Tayeh*   183
My hair is my identity *by Raed Sadi*   189
How Gaza inspired me to be a 'surgeon' for
   historic buildings *by Eman Shawwa*   192
The nightmare that is online shopping
   (in Gaza) *by Akram Abunahla*   197
Long live sunny Friday mornings *by Butien Riman*   202

CHAPTER SEVEN
2021

A degree in surviving assaults *by Basman Derawi*   209
Love is more than a family name *by Orjwan Shurrab*   211
The donkey carts of Gaza *by Hassan Alalami*   214
Flashbacks of smoke and solidarity
   by Hanan Abukmail   217

CHAPTER EIGHT
2022

My home *by Eman Alhaj Ali*	223
Interrupted graduation *by Aseel Zeineddin*	225
Art for more than the eyes *by Ahmed Alsammak*	229
One day in Gazan life *by Israa Mohammed Jamal*	233

CHAPTER NINE
2023 (January–October)

The perennials *by Eman Alhaj Ali*	241
Who will pay for the twenty years we lost? *by Yousef Maher Dawas*	243
A lost sibling and a resurrection *by Eman Alhaj Ali*	248
A Palestinian woman takes charge *by Lubna Abuhashem*	251
Does creativity only come from misery? *by Dana Besaiso*	254
Dreaming of Palestinian planes in the sky *by Shahd Safi*	258

CHAPTER TEN
October 2023–Present

Echoes of Gaza, from afar *by Basma Almaza*	267

I've been displaced from two homes. Now I'm waiting for a third *by Maram Faraj*	272
I search for food and water all day, then we're told to flee; yet no place is safe *by Hamza Ibrahim*	279
The sight of stars makes me dream *by Roaa Missmeh*	285
I'm determined to run towards the sun *by Reem Sleem*	287
I miss you, my brother *by Mahmoud Alyazji*	291
A mother's journey through war *by Orjwan Shurrab*	294
The flour massacre *by Ahmed Dader*	301
Love amid chaos *by Samah Abushaibah*	305
Searching for my missing friend *by Alaa Mahdi Kudaih*	308
Where is our home? *by Wejdan Wajdy Abu Shammala*	312
My Black Friday *by Yusuf El-Mbayed*	318
A wedding and condolences *by Tala Herzallah*	325
Gaza, my homeland, we will rebuild you one day *by Aya Zaqout*	328
Tell Them *by Huda Skaik*	333
Epilogue *by Ahmed Alnaouq and Pam Bailey*	338
Acknowledgements	343

We Are Not Numbers

Introduction: the 'birth' of We Are Not Numbers
by Ahmed Alnaouq and Pam Bailey

It was the autumn of 2014, just days after a ceasefire ended what was then Israel's worst assault on Gaza yet. Just like after the two other major wars before it, and a number of other less severe offensives, hope was struggling to gain a footing – hope that this time, the truce would be followed by an international push not only for reconstruction, but to assure Palestinians' independence and basic human rights.

We knew it was probably a pipe dream, but still we hoped.

Pam was in Washington, DC, unable to return to Gaza after spending the better part of three years in what she considered her second home, working as an activist, freelance journalist and independent teacher of English and social media skills (much in demand during the height of the Arab Spring). Raised by a family committed to social justice and trained initially as a print journalist, Pam had taken a significant departure from her upbringing by becoming a vice president for a large corporate conglomerate. After realising the role didn't reflect her values, she knew she needed a reboot.

The invitation from CODEPINK, an American anti-war organisation, to join a women's delegation to Gaza in early 2009 offered the pivotal change she sought. One trip to Gaza led to another, and a lasting commitment to the people and the culture blossomed. Shunning the hotels and guarded apartments typically preferred by foreign agency workers and journalists, Pam chose to live with families. One evening, at a birthday party, she briefly met a young man named Ahmed Alnaouq.

Like most of the other young people at the gathering, Ahmed was studying English literature at university – the best way to master a language required to land a good-paying job with one of the international NGOs and perhaps secure a scholarship to study abroad. But with a shortage of native English-speaking teachers (a 'gift' of the Israeli blockade), mastering the written language was difficult. Pam and Ahmed kept in touch via Facebook in the months that followed.

Then came Israel's launch of Operation Protective Edge on 8 July 2014.

Ahmed was raised in Deir al-Balah, a community in the middle of the Gaza Strip. With three brothers and five sisters, Ahmed grew up in a tightly knit family. But he was closest to Ayman, the handsome and charismatic big brother Ahmed most wanted to emulate. Ayman was a natural leader who soon became a needed provider for his struggling family, securing a scarce job as an accountant with an established non-governmental organisation. He was, quite simply, the family's hope.

On 19 July 2014, Ayman and four of his best friends were killed by an Israeli missile. In an instant everything changed, submerging Ahmed in a darkness so black he couldn't find his way out.

Usually a prolific poster on Facebook, Ahmed went silent. His profile picture was replaced by Ayman's.

Pam noticed and sent him a message. 'Ahmed, are you OK?'

'I'm fine,' he responded.

'No. Tell me something real,' Pam replied.

He told her the truth: he was not OK. But after the usual condolences *(I'm so sorry for your loss . . .)* Pam leaned into the tragedy.

'I wish I had known Ayman,' Pam wrote. 'Tell me about him. What are some of your favourite memories?'

Being a writer herself and knowing that Ahmed (like most of the young Palestinians she met in Gaza) wanted to work on his English, she went a step further.

'Write a story about him. We can work on it together,' she said.

Over the next three months, they passed the 'story of Ayman' back and forth. Pam encouraged Ahmed to share specific anecdotes that would bring Ayman to life. But she could tell Ahmed was holding something back. As she gently probed, Ahmed revealed that after years of humiliation and torment from the Israeli occupation and blockade, his older brother had joined the Palestinian liberation movement. That is why Ayman was targeted that fateful day, and why Ahmed feared Pam would now consider his brother a terrorist. But by that point Pam had come to know Ayman as a brother, son and fiancé: a kind, hard-working, passionate young man who felt driven to somehow protect his family and his people.

When the story was complete, they recognised that a sort of magic had happened. Ahmed's written English had improved more in the three months they had worked together than it had in the last year in university. In the process, his feeling of hopelessness had begun to lift. At the same time, Pam gained an insight into the human impact of historical events she had not yet fully grasped. And together, they produced a story that could educate and – even more importantly – *move* a Western public that largely treated Palestinians, particularly those who resist, as stereotypes. They had also forged a transcontinental friendship that has lasted more than a decade.

'There are so many young people in Gaza who have lost loved ones due to the Israeli assault. What if we recreated for them the magic Ahmed and I found?' Pam wrote one day to a few friends and supporters.

This was how the idea for We Are Not Numbers (now often called simply WANN) was 'hatched'. But every idea needs advocates and resources to become

INTRODUCTION

real. The guardian angel who helped WANN transform from an idea to reality was Ramy Abdu, who Pam had met earlier and had founded his own organisation, the Euro-Mediterranean Human Rights Monitor. Ramy, and later his team, offered office space, the initial salary for a project manager, funds to build a website and on-the-ground oversight of the staff in Gaza as it slowly grew (especially after Pam was deported from Gaza by Israel in 2016 and banned from returning). Later, as the Israeli grip on Gaza tightened, Ramy managed to leave for Turkey, and now also is not allowed to return. Ahmed, who became WANN's third project manager and is now the international director, finally was able to quench his thirst to see the world when he secured a prestigious Chevening scholarship to study in the United Kingdom. He too is now not able to return. That is the agonising price of travelling out of Gaza. Too often, it's a one-way door.

Another early collaborator was Refaat Alareer, the beloved English professor and author, who signed on as both adviser and instructor for the youths who answered the call and applied to join WANN.

Equally as important were the writing coaches recruited from around the world, professional authors, teachers, journalists and communications professionals, who have agreed – without pay – to serve as mentors for the 'WAN-Ners'. Pam and Ahmed knew that, along the way, many of them would become close friends with their mentees, like Pam had. The mentors would help alleviate the young people's isolation and serve as their champions. (And that has proven to be true. Mentors have provided job references, helped the writers win scholarships abroad and – now, in the wake of the genocide – helped raise money to escape to Egypt or abroad and support their families.)

Members of We Are Not Numbers are aspiring writers aged eighteen to twenty-nine – a large but often neglected group that is hit hardest by unemployment and despair. Twenty-one per cent of Gaza's population is between fifteen and twenty-four years old, and before the genocide began, an estimated 60 per cent of them were unemployed. Before this latest war destroyed the universities, many young people majored in English literature, in the hope that they would earn a better-paying job at an international NGO or secure a coveted international scholarship. When they graduated from university, however, finding a way to use their skills to earn a decent income and pursue their dreams was impossible for many.

Our mission with WANN was to create a new generation of Palestinian writers and thinkers, who could harness the power of their words to non-violently resist their oppression and influence public opinion about the ongoing Israeli blockade of Gaza. WANN provides the world with direct access to Palestinian narratives without censorship or intermediaries.

The first stories (after Ahmed's) began to be published on the We Are Not Numbers website in May

INTRODUCTION

2015. From 2015 to 2024, more than 1,300 stories were mentored and published by 323 young adult Palestinians.

This book is a selection of some of the best WANN essays and poems over a span of ten years – a unique, living history of Gaza as seen through the eyes of its youth. It was extremely difficult to narrow down the selection to what you find on these pages. We regret having to omit so many heartfelt and often surprisingly hopeful narratives. We encourage you to visit the We Are Not Numbers website to read them all.

Our members write about everything from death, homelessness and the search for scarce electricity, to pleasures large and small like *tashas* (gatherings) by the sea and the birth of a new family member. As you explore their fears and dreams, you'll come full circle. We Are Not Numbers was created in a time of war, and here we are again. Only this time, during the massive Israeli assault that began in October 2023, *twenty-one* members of Ahmed's family were killed. An early-morning air strike left only him and two sisters to continue the clan's legacy. Ahmed watched helplessly from his new home in London.

There are other ways that this war is different from 2014: its sheer duration (at the time of writing, it is over five times longer than Operation Protective Edge) and the unrelenting obliteration of entire neighbourhoods, civic institutions and the professionals needed to rebuild: teachers (including Refaat Alareer), physicians, law-enforcement professionals and more. The Israeli plan seems to be more like ethnic cleansing than the crushing of Hamas.

The following chapters are organised by year, beginning with the project's formal founding in 2015. Reading the stories and poems over time will give you a feel for the 'ebb and flow' of Gazan life – not only the near-constant Israeli assaults (many people don't realise how common they have been, outside of the major operations), but also everyday challenges and pleasures. And then there are the stories from 2023 and 2024, which some may want to read first, to better understand the events that have been so much in the news. The views that follow in this collection are the real voices of young people that often go unheard.

At the end of each essay, we share an update on each writer, since so much has happened since they first shared their story or poem. However, these updates are current only until this writing, in November 2024.

The stories from We Are Not Numbers show two truths that cannot be denied: the extent to which WANN's members are like young people everywhere, with the same hopes and passions, and the significant talent they could contribute – if they were simply allowed to thrive. Among our original cohort of writers, many have realised their dreams despite the barriers erected by the Israeli blockade and international inaction: Mosab Abu Toha is now an internationally acclaimed poet and essayist, Said Alyacoubi is a surgeon in the UK, Issam

INTRODUCTION

Adwan was hired as a journalist by the Associated Press, and Hind Khoudary is a journalist with Al Jazeera.

It is these young people, and their determination to keep sharing their stories, who offer hope for the future.

> *If I must die,*
> *you must live*
> *to tell my story.*
> *Let it bring hope,*
> *let it be a tale.*
>
> – Refaat Alareer, 'If I Must Die'

CHAPTER ONE

2015

Ayman: to the world a number; to me, my brother and best friend
by Ahmed Alnaouq, mentored by Pam Bailey

28 January 1991 was an extremely happy day for my family: after four years of trying (and four sisters!) my mother finally delivered a second boy. My parents named him Ayman, which means 'righteous'. Mom used to say she didn't believe happiness could cause people to cry, but when Ayman was born, she discovered it was true. She was so happy that she dressed him in gold, which is not usually accepted in an Islamic society.

My mom let it be known that no one was allowed to hit Ayman. If he beat up anyone, the victim would just have to take it silently or walk away; if he broke a favourite vase or bowl in his rambunctiousness at home, she cleaned it up and didn't say a word.

Ayman's reputation as a 'golden child' continued in school. His teachers called him 'prince' due to his kindness and good manners. He became well known for his smile; he smiled even in bad situations.

But then came the Second Intifada in 2000, and Ayman was exposed directly to death for the first time. While he was playing with his friends, an Israeli tank stopped in the middle of the road, opening fire – killing five of his friends and injuring around eleven others.

It was Ayman's fate to hide behind a wall, and he was saved. Their only crime was to come into the path of the tank! They just wanted to play like other kids.

From that point on, happenings like this occurred frequently, not only with Ayman, but with so many other Palestinian kids. That was – and is – life in Gaza. But we could do nothing, and that ate at Ayman.

When the intifada ended five years later, we knew we were fortunate to have survived. Hundreds of Palestinians were killed and injured, and thousands of homes were demolished. And the peace didn't last long. In 2008, Israel launched the first of its major wars on Gaza, seeming to us like it was intent on killing every breathing thing. It did not differentiate resisters from civilians. Israeli soldiers killed more than 1,300 people and injured more than 5,000, most of them civilians. Yet they claimed the war was only against Hamas, the party and social movement that also is the government.

During that war on Gaza, Ayman was still in high school. He saw his friends both die and grieve. More than 340 kids like him were killed. Ayman was an eyewitness to it all. He was only seventeen. He was unable to concentrate enough to study, yet he continued to get good marks.

When the war ended, the Israeli army tightened its blockade of Gaza. We could not obtain gas, water, oil or electricity. Conditions were especially difficult for our family; we suffered a lot because my father was a taxi driver and he could not find fuel for his car. This blockade took us back hundreds of years; we even needed firewood to cook.

Ayman finally found a way to become active in standing up for his family and his people, working with an organisation that allowed him to get aid for needy people and distribute it in our neighbourhood. In times of misfortune, the neighbours came to Ayman; they thought he was the only hope.

He also joined the UN's Gaza Training Centre, studying for a financial management diploma. Ayman graduated after just two years; his certificate was our hope to escape the poverty that pulled us down. Finally, a year later, Ayman found a job as an accountant for the Association of Construction and Relief. It was a momentous day.

In 2012, Israel again invaded our land for eight seemingly endless days. When it was over, Ayman was not the same. He was restless, desperate to find a more effective way to protect his people and defend his homeland.

In the meantime, my father became ill and required open-heart surgery. He could no longer work, so Ayman was our family's only support. (My oldest brother was now married and could barely support his own family.) He walked to work, thus saving a little money. Ayman gave all his salary to my father, so he could take care of our family's needs.

Despite our reliance on Ayman, my mother did her best to convince him to marry. She wanted Ayman to be happy, and to her, that meant he must start his own family. After a while, he agreed, and Mother hurried to engage him to a suitable girl. Ayman started to prepare a flat to live in. But it was not to be.

In July 2014, Israel launched its third war on Gaza. From the beginning, the Israeli army struck houses of civilians. It demolished many vital institutions, including hospitals, schools and mosques. They tested all kinds of internationally prohibited weapons on us and, in the process, exterminated entire families. Even dead people were not safe; graveyards were bombed and bones were exposed. Gaza was sinking in the blood of families and children.

Ayman's rage grew inside him. Since no other type of resistance seemed to work, he joined an armed wing of Palestinians. On 19 July 2014, he was with five of his friends in a building ravaged by a previous war when a missile weighing thousands of kilogrammes obliterated their gathering place – causing his soul to fly to its creator. Ayman was gone. And so were our dreams.

When I close my eyes, I see his face. How can I forget him? He was always by my side, never leaving me even when I was in trouble. He died and left my mother cracked in pieces. He died and left my father weeping all night long.

Every day, when I see Ayman's friends who are still alive, I feel a bitterness of loss I cannot bear.

Ahmed's father was born in 1948 a few months after the Nakba, when 750,000 Palestinians were driven from their homes in what is now Israel. His mother,

Basema, died of breast cancer in 2020, a victim of a blockade that denies residents advanced medical care. On 22 October 2023, an Israeli bombardment killed twenty-one of Ahmed's family members: his father, Nasri Alnaouq, aged seventy-five; sister, Walaa, thirty-six, and her children (Ragd, thirteen, Eslam, twelve, Sara, nine, and Abdullah, six); brother, Muhammad, thirty-five, and his children (Bakr, eleven, and Basema, nine); sister, Alaa, thirty-five, and her children (Eslam, thirteen, Dima, twelve, Tala, eight, Noor, four, and Nasmah, two); sister, Aya, thirty-three, and her children (Malak Bashir, twelve, Mohammed Bashir, nine, and Tamin Bashir, six); cousin, Ali Alqurinwi, thirty-five; and Ahmed's younger brother, Mahmoud Alnaouq, twenty-five (who wrote one of the essays in Chapter 4 of this book). Later many more cousins were killed and Ahmed continues to be in exile from his homeland.

An ode to my roof, the thin line between life and death
by Haya Abu Shammala, mentored by Alice Bach

Last night, I stayed awake until morning studying for the next day's exam. Yes, I'm lazy. I could have learned the material the day before. But I delay tasks as if waiting for them to get done by themselves. A year has passed since the 2014 Israeli war on Gaza, and I still can't seem to keep up with life, including studying for my exams.

Trying to relieve my exhaustion, I closed my eyes, rested my head on the back of my chair, and breathed in and out. When I opened my eyes, we exchanged glances. Almost one year has passed since the first day of the last war, when we became friends. You were the first thing I saw in the morning and the last thing I saw at night. *Good morning, my roof*, I'd say. Then, *Good night, my friend. Will this be the last time? Will I survive the coming night?*

Each day, I convinced myself that my roof would protect me from the chaos around me. I needed someone or something I could speak to about the craziness in my head, without being accused of losing my mind. My mom told me when I was young: 'Once you ignore the monster under your bed, it will leave you alone.' Fake it till you make it. I thought if I ignored the war roaring out there, the Israelis would withdraw and simply let us live.

2015

What is worse than expecting to die at any moment? Sometimes I envy the dead because they don't have to wait any more. Fear is a more effective weapon than rockets; it leaves its victims haunted by the possible scenarios of how and when they will be killed. Every night, I asked my roof, *Will you ever collapse on me?*

When it became too scary to look at the sky because it was full of drones, my roof became my sky. I imagined it to be the serene blue I love – although, during the war, I lost my appreciation for colour. Almost everything looked grey to me. My roof and the room below became my refuge. I needed more layers to hide within. I longed to disappear, to be forgotten. All I wanted was to skip this chapter of the story. Let me move forward!

The roof witnessed the nights I spent crying, trying to melt my fear away in the salty tears. We spent hours together, imagining life after the nightmare finally ended. I could almost hear the roof burst out laughing the day my friend called and told me she had to survive because she had bought new shoes the day before the war started, and she couldn't die with them unworn. The roof also heard me and my family discussing whether to evacuate our home because our neighbourhood was not safe any more. Would it feel abandoned? On other nights, the roof and I were silent, staring at each other.

Sometimes I thought about all the other people throughout history who probably spent their nights staring at their roofs, wishing the next bomb would not be their fate. What goodbyes and I love yous they must have witnessed, sharing moments of repentance, sorrow, joy and relief. Roofs are sounding boards for stories that end up never being told. Roofs are the thin line between life and death, between drones above and people waiting to be killed beneath.

I'm not very experienced in life, but after living through three Israeli wars against Gaza, I know that nobody truly survives a war. Wars either kill you or leave you among the walking wounded. Sometimes it's hard to know what living really means.

Once, a missile hit our neighbourhood, and I only knew I was still living because my roof was still there. When last summer's war against Gaza ended, some parts of my home were damaged. And I noticed that cracks were spreading like spiders across my roof. Finally, I realised the great burden even my roof had to bear.

Nothing truly survives a war.

Haya left Gaza for Qatar before the war to earn her master's degree in translation studies. She has found work there in communications and public relations. She lives and works in Qatar, where she also earned her master's degree. Her family, who remain in Gaza, are forever in her mind and heart.

A chance encounter with my teacher – and a tree
by Allam Zedan, mentored by Greta Berlin

He had the same smile. I wanted to hug him and tell him that I missed him. I missed his classes. I missed the wisdom he taught us, the experience he gave us. 'Do you know me?' I asked.

He looked at me intently, scrutinising the man standing in front of him. 'You are that little kid who used to torture me, wanting to answer every question I asked,' he said and smiled again. That smile took me back years. I remembered that he lived here in Beit Hanoun. This was his home. Over there is the tree he inherited from his father, although its branches are now covered in grey, sticky dust. For the first time in my life, I didn't know what to say. War had killed life in this town.

There are no more birds here. I'd come here many times before, but this time was different. Everything was different. His passion was to help his students navigate through life and help his country thrive. But my teacher had nothing left on this land, part of a former state that is recognised only in ancient history, where nothing like Israel existed.

He pinched my ear the way he did when I was a child in fifth grade and paying no attention. He reminded me that I used to sit in front of him with a packet of sunflower seeds, hiding them under my desk and eating them surreptitiously. 'What has happened to you, Allam? How have you become the man now standing in front of me?'

'I enrolled in university, studied for a bachelor's in Arabic language, and received a technical diploma in translation; here I am, however.' My eyes couldn't bear looking at him.

I know it makes you sad, my teacher. I know I am a great disappointment. I tried my best to be who you hoped I could be. I studied hard. Yet I am from the Gaza Strip. I really tried to get a job. I even tried to be a freelancer. Guess what? I can't open a checking account unless I am a businessman or an employee of an international company. The fate of young adults like me is to die or languish. I am the generation who has lived through three wars.

He told me that the first sixty years of a human's life are difficult, but things get easier afterwards. I laughed. He laughed too. 'What about your son, Laith? How is he doing?' I asked. 'I knew him when we were in a boring class together. He was the one who always turned it into a festival.'

My teacher wept.

Don't say it, please. Don't tell me he was killed. I have enough pain in my life. I lost many friends during the Israeli aggression against Gaza last summer. Don't say it, teacher, please. Don't.

With tears in his eyes, he smiled and said: 'Oh, Allam. My son was such a good boy. I still remember his laughter. His jokes. His . . . everything. He used to fill our life with happiness. My son was killed by the first Israeli shell that struck our home. His blood was everywhere. He left us.'

I didn't have any words to say to him. All I could think was 'I am so sorry.' I shouldn't have asked him about my friend, his son. I should've stayed silent. The sight of the rubble lying on the ground, the smell of death filling the air and the pulse of pain in his eyes should've silenced me. I should have known.

Then, he told me he had a surprise for me. 'What is it, teacher?'

'I avenged my son's murder.'

I started to think he had gone crazy after the death of his son. How the hell did he avenge his son's murder? This didn't make any sense to me, and I was afraid to ask, but I did.

'And how did you do that?'

'They stole my son from me, but my wife is pregnant with another child,' he replied. I smiled, knowing that this man is a survivor. It had been a long time since I attended his classes, yet he had a last lesson to teach me. 'Don't give up, Allam. Be patient and stay to fight another day.'

Allam still lives in Gaza, and before the genocide began he ran a successful translation business. Shortly before this writing, he was forced out of his home in Jabalia, a community in northern Gaza, by Israeli forces. He hopes to leave Gaza with his wife and daughter as soon as the border opens, to create a new life.

What makes life worth living?
by Anas Jnena, mentored by Leslie Thatcher

I first met Ahmed* in early 2012, in a small park in Gaza's Shujaiya neighbourhood – a place where my friends and I usually meet whenever there is a power cut in our neighbourhood. The night air was dry and cool, and I was waiting for my friends to arrive. On that day, however, they were late. While I waited, I sat on a rock with a flat surface at the corner of the park and lost myself in a sea of thoughts. I was planning a prank to scare one of my best friends, Hamza.

In the darkness, I saw someone approaching, and immediately thought of Hamza. I could already feel the excitement deep in the pit of my stomach as I imagined his face when I pulled my prank on him. But much to my surprise, it was someone else.

That was our first meeting. He said hello; I returned his greeting. He looked calm and wise, but he was not the educated type. His features were not what you would call typically handsome, but there was something about his face that captured my attention. I loved the way he smiled; it was sort of crooked, his black eyes seemed to

---

* *Not the WANN co-founder, Ahmed Alnaouq.*

shrink, and his lips curved inward as if he was sucking on a lemon. Even today, whenever I see Ahmed smile, I know it is genuine and not forced. Since Hamza hadn't arrived yet – though he had promised me he would be on time – I struck up a conversation with Ahmed. And his story was unexpected.

Ahmed is the second-oldest child among ten. He dropped out of school when he was fifteen. His parents struggled to keep the family afloat, so he decided he too should work. He started selling newspapers on the streets.

Unemployment is very high in Gaza; nearly 60 per cent among the youth. But Ahmed soon was lucky enough to land a better-paying job – as a worker in the smuggling tunnels of Rafah, in the southern part of Gaza, beneath the Egyptian border. Those smuggling tunnels employed thousands of young men whose job was mainly to haul goods – including food, clothing and fuel – into the blockaded Gaza. The work was hard and dangerous; he was assigned a twelve-hour shift, six days a week, in cramped spaces. Sudden tunnel collapses, electrocution and Israeli air strikes were very possible. However, that didn't stop Ahmed from being a diligent worker. He was grateful for the work; the pay was around 150 shekels (£25) per day, and he knew that with this job, he could ensure the ones he loved a better future.

On some days, Ahmed spent the night at his workplace, since his home was relatively far from Rafah. He often found shelter at the entrance of the tunnel and tried his best to get the rest his body desperately needed. Although it wasn't comfortable sleeping on the ground, far from home in a place where his life was endangered, Ahmed never minded much.

Most of his earnings were used for his family's expenses, but instead of grumbling about not having much for himself – as most youths our age do – Ahmed instead felt that he had accomplished something big in life. He even gave around £1,200 to his oldest brother for his marriage. I had never encountered someone so selfless, and we became close friends.

Early the next year (2013), Ahmed finally got engaged to the girl he loved. Perhaps God had listened to his silent prayers. He even brought me and some friends some sweets and invited us to dinner. Seeing Ahmed happy brought light to everyone's heart. But getting engaged also changed Ahmed a bit. He worked twice as hard as he had before. Many of his friends didn't see him that often any more, since he was always too busy with work.

Later that year, the unexpected happened. Egypt's military destroyed most of the smuggling tunnels to improve their own security, causing Ahmed and thousands of other young Gazans to lose their humble jobs. The transition from employed to unemployed changed Ahmed's life in many ways. He started to spend most of his time in Shujaiya Park, feeling more and more pessimistic and hopeless. He delayed his wedding celebration because he couldn't afford the expenses. Money that he earned from odd jobs went to his family. Day by day, his financial situation became worse.

By 2014, Ahmed couldn't bring himself to visit his fiancée's house because he felt so ashamed. If he didn't even have money to provide for his current family, how could he support a wife and family? He felt as if the world had turned sinister and now was laughing at his failure. One cold and dry night, after the power went out, Ahmed decided to put an end to his suffering. He found an electric cable and tied it to the ceiling of his room. Ahmed got up on the chair and kicked it away.

But his life did not end there.

As if on cue, his sister found Ahmed hanging and screamed. Her cries echoed through the house, waking everyone. Mohammed, Ahmed's younger brother, appeared in a flash – lifting him up to relieve the tension while his sister cut the cable. Ahmed was miraculously saved.

As for me, I could not suppress my confusion and doubt. I asked him directly: 'Why did you do it, Ahmed?' He replied: 'Because I no longer have any self-esteem. All doors of hope have been closed to me in Gaza. Unemployment is like a living death.'

Today, Anas lives and works as a teacher in Kuwait. However, the rest of his family remain trapped in Gaza. His father was killed during the genocide and a brother was gravely injured.

An explosion of a different kind: Gaza in colour
by Nada Hammad, mentored by Tom Sperlinger

Gaza looked like a canvas of grey after Israel's Operation Protective Edge was over. Thousands of houses crumbled to the ground. Farms bloomed with ashes instead of their usual vibrant green. Sometimes there were splashes of red and maroon mixed in, from blood spilled on the roads after a night of heavy bombing.

It started small. All healing does. A grey wall painted white. A wall with colourful graffiti swirling around its holes and cracks. Phrases like *Gaza will never die, Long live the resistance* and *We salute the steadfastness of the people of Gaza* were painted in vivid colours all over Gaza. They were a declaration of survival, a burning will to live despite the destruction. Everywhere you turned, you saw small splashes of colour – vivid colours that weren't meant to mask the grey, but rather share its space. It was a declaration of survival, not a struggle to forget.

The artists in Gaza, however, needed something bigger, something that screamed hope instead of whispering it on small roads and narrow walls. This is when the Colours of Hope campaign started. Some of Gaza's people who were left homeless after the war were given small, modular houses. These 'caravans' looked dull, uniform and, above all, lifeless. Each time you saw one of them you were reminded of a destroyed home, a lost haven. Many of Gaza's artists noticed the sadness that clung to these caravans and decided to act.

They painted the caravan walls vibrant blues, oranges and reds. To make them even more lively, the artists added drawings of eyes, parrots and leaves. The artwork didn't paint over the inhabitants' loss or the difficulties they faced every day, but they offered a window of hope with a glimpse of a brighter future.

After the portable homes, the artists' thirst for colours grew. Gaza's sea port, al-Mina, is one of the first places people go to relax and breathe some fresh air (although it's often fishy). It is almost always packed with people of all ages – kids running and playing, young men and women gazing at the horizon or chatting with friends, old people passing the time with the sea for company.

It took the artists five days to finish painting the port's walls with a rainbow of colours. Some of the fishermen rushed to help them once they realised why all the paint buckets had been lugged to the seaport. Dalia Abdelrahman, the campaign's coordinator and head artist, said: 'Ever since Gaza's seaport was opened to the public after the fighting, the cracked cement walls and the boulders lying around reminded me of the war's destruction. I thought to myself, *Why don't we colour them up and turn them into something beautiful?* I contacted some donors and fellow artists to work out what could be done and that's how it started.'

Earlier this year, my dad took us on a road trip along the coast, from the seafront in Jabalia to the edges of Rafah city. One of our stops was al-Mina, because my younger siblings had not seen it yet. As he was driving along the seaport's narrow, sandy road, I pointed out to my sister, Nour, all the graffiti painted on the walls. We asked Dad to pull over so we could get out and see the artwork up close. Everywhere I turned, I was met with colours. As we walked, a large, intricate expanse of graffiti grabbed my attention. It was a line from Marcel Khalife's famous song 'My Homeland' (*Ya Watani*, in Arabic). The line says: 'I have chosen you, oh my homeland.'

An initiative called Colour Your Neighbourhood (*Lawwen Hartak*, in Arabic) was the next step. The colouring took place just before the holy month of Ramadan.

'The idea started with a Facebook discussion between a few of us,' Salsabeel Zeineddin, a WANN writer and one of the young women who participated in the campaign, told me. 'We had seen many pictures of beautifully coloured cities outside Gaza on the internet. Those pictures showed just how big a difference a paint bucket can make for a house or a town. And since Gaza has a right to some of this colourful beauty, we decided to do it.'

The campaign's participants were mostly young women from Gaza. In our culture, it was unusual at first to see women in the street, painting, doing what many perceive as a man's job. Salsabeel noted: 'At the beginning, neighbourhood residents were taken aback by us and our paint buckets, but after they saw the colours and the effort we were putting in, they started to help us. I jumped with joy. It felt as if all the negative energy I had bottled up through the past year was vanishing with every brush stroke.'

The joy that colours can bring to one's life is truly magical. I try to incorporate colour everywhere in my life. My backpacks are adorned with smiley-face buttons. My notebook has stickers stuck to its plain black cover. My prized and well-loved pen cases are filled to the brim with coloured markers.

My friends ask me why I bother with the stickers and coloured pens when I'm clearly not in primary or middle school any more. I tell them that colours make me happy. Happiness is a choice. It is also a process of trial and error, and above all of perseverance. The participants of each one of these campaigns wanted to give Gaza and its people hope in the way they know best – in colour.

Nada is a teacher, translator and content writer who is struggling to survive the ongoing genocide in Gaza. She is a single mom, daughter and sister, who dreams of a better future for herself and her family. She is waiting for the Egyptian border to open to be able to evacuate with the rest of her family to safety in Egypt.

A flower grows from wreckage
by Ismail Abu-Aitah, mentored by Pam Bailey

No matter how hard life is, a family who support you through the good and the bad give you the strength to overcome. That certainly is true for me. I come from a family of eleven: parents, four boys and five girls. And although we were always poor (only one – my brother Mahmoud – had a full-time job, as a policeman), I considered myself truly blessed.

Then came July 2014. On 8 July that year, life in Gaza was turned upside down. Israel unleashed its rockets, tanks and other human-killing machines on a population struggling just to put food on their tables due to the strangling blockade. Injuries and deaths were reported so quickly we lost count. Most of them were civilians. Yes, we believe in our right to resist Israel's oppression by any means necessary, but the vast majority of Gaza's residents are merely trying to make a living with dignity.

Then, on 24 July, my family joined the statistics, and my life for ever changed.

My brothers Mohammed, Mahmoud and I ate a meal with our family after a long, tiring day at work. It was Ramadan, a holy Muslim month of fasting. And like the previous four years, the three of us made and sold *qatayef*, a special dessert commonly eaten during Ramadan. Despite the escalating Israeli assault, we had fun; everyone smiled and the kids played around us. After three major wars in six years, children in Gaza have learned how to pretend that tanks and F-16s are not outside, flying low overhead. Such is our dysfunctional life in Gaza.

Close to midnight, everyone was preparing for sleep. I remember my dad readying himself for the *Fajr* (dawn) prayer. My brothers left for home with their wives and children (I have twenty nieces and nephews!), and my mom came to chat with me in my room. She told me about a poem she had heard and loved and asked me to listen. It was in the middle of that poem, now etched in my brain for ever, that a huge, roaring sound rattled the entire area. I woke my dad and the rest of the family, and we all headed downstairs towards the ground floor, thinking it would be the safest place.

The next thing I remember is waking up in Shifa Hospital (Gaza City). Confused, I asked about Mom, Dad and the rest of my family. The doctors said they were OK, and the relief of knowing they were safe was all that mattered to me; I could handle my own pain.

Shrapnel had lacerated my entire body, and I had suffered a severe concussion. The doctors took X-rays, cleaned and stitched my wounds, and put me to bed for rest. Meanwhile, I briefly saw my third brother, Mahmoud, who also was hospitalised for treatment. He was discharged quickly, but I stayed due to my head trauma.

At noon on my first full day in the hospital, a few of

my friends visited. I was in tremendous pain and couldn't move. Yet I was happy because I felt I had somehow taken a hit for my family, sparing their lives. But after a short while, one of my friends broke the news. Despite my uncles' hesitancy to tell me, they had decided I deserved to know: an air strike, which had targeted our neighbour's house, had badly damaged my own home and killed five of my family members: my mom, Jamila; my dad, Ibrahim; my two brothers, Mohammed and Ahmed; and my four-year-old nephew, Adham. Ten other family members were wounded.

Everything went black. I jumped out of bed and begged my friends to take me to Kamal Adwan Hospital, where they said my family's bodies were being held. I needed to see them before they were buried. I could not have lived with the pain if I had not. Somehow, despite my injuries, I made it there and kissed their heads, hands and cheeks, except for my mom's. I was told it was inappropriate to uncover her in the presence of men, and I believed them. In retrospect, I don't know how I feel; her physical condition was so bad that perhaps it is best that it was not my last memory of her.

I didn't want to leave their side, but my friends forced me to take care of myself and took me back to Shifa Hospital. During the following three days in bed, I blamed myself for what happened. Irrationally, I thought that if I hadn't woken up my family members, it would have turned out differently. I was so angry that I wasn't among those who died. Why should I live?

Later, I visited my thirteen-year-old sister Alaa, who suffered a skull fracture, brain haemorrhage, internal bleeding and a double fracture in her left leg. She asked me in a trembling voice: 'Where is Mom? I want Mom!' I lied to her and said she was wounded. I left the room, sat on the floor and cried. I had no choice but to lie. Her condition was serious and such devastating news would break a mountain into pieces, let alone a person.

I also visited my sisters-in-law, who were badly injured and in the same hospital. One of them, a mother of two sons and a daughter, asked about her family. Again, I lied and said they were fine. I concealed the news that we had lost her husband (my brother) and her youngest son.

When I was finally discharged, I returned to my home to see what had become of the place of my youth. Shocked at what I saw, I sat down in the middle of the street and sobbed. When I entered the house and saw blood everywhere, I collapsed.

I was put in a car and taken to my sister Elham's house to recover for a few days. I stayed there for two weeks, then insisted on returning to clean the place up, despite the fact that my injuries had not yet healed and the war was still raging.

Have you ever felt as if you were alive and dead at the same time? That is how I felt – like I had died with my family in the blast, even though I was still breathing.

Only recently have I got back on my feet and started to feel again. I am now responsible for three younger sisters, and I also must help my two sisters-in-law raise their children, who have lost their fathers. I must repair the damage inflicted on my house by the explosion. I turned down a four-year master's and PhD scholarship from the University of South Carolina. I still cannot find a job. The worst part is the fear that I won't be able to live up to my responsibilities.

It is now 24 July once again, a year later. Once again, I am working through Ramadan selling *qatayef*. It is excruciating to be in the same place, doing an activity I shared with my brother Mohammed last year. In some ways, I am still in disbelief and denial. It's as if I am living in a loop: one day repeating itself over and over. I have lost track of time, days, months, years.

I try to escape by helping others, mainly by listening to my sisters and sisters-in-law as they vent their own grief. I try to escape by working on the house: repainting, redecorating, refurnishing. I am choosing to look at pain as wreckage from which a flower can still grow. My youngest sister, Alaa, is working hard to become a doctor, and as she attends high school, I am eager for her to become a person my mom, dad, Mohammed, Ahmed and Adham would be very proud of.

Then came 7 October 2023 and the ensuing Israeli war on Gaza. Ismail – now married, with three children (the youngest four months old) – was forced to relocate five times, under heavy shelling.

Thankfully, he didn't lose any more immediate family members. But about a hundred relatives are among the dead. The bright spot in all the blackness is that Ismail's sister Alaa graduated from medical school in Egypt in December 2024.

A book lover's simple dream
by Khaled Alostath, mentored by Catherine Baker

Last year, I read about a hundred novels, and all of them were in PDF format. So far this year, I have finished 152 novels (plus about ten nonfiction books), all of them also in PDF format. If you have tried to read an entire book in PDF form, you know it's very awkward for pleasure reading. (Yes, I know a lot of foreigners love their Kindles, but we don't have them or even many iPads here in Gaza. Try reading books on your laptop or mobile phone. But even if I had one of the new digital devices made just for reading, I am pretty sure I'd prefer a paper book.)

I don't want to read books this way, but I have no other choice. In Gaza, we have no free library where people can check out books. We have two bookstores, but it's beyond my budget to buy as many books as this avid reader could consume. It helps that I have a good friend who also loves to read; we make sure that when we buy books, we select different ones so we can exchange them.

My friend and I are not the only people in Gaza who are in love with reading. Because of the scarcity of hard copies, most of us must read online or from PDF print-outs, rather than curling up with a book in our hands.

This is a problem because we have electricity for less than eight hours a day, and when we do have power, it typically comes on after 11 p.m. If you fall asleep before then – which happens most of the time, especially in winter – you miss the opportunity to recharge your laptop, and you may not be able to read again until the next night.

In Gaza, there is a coffee shop called Cordoba that has a small library for its patrons. Most of the books are in Arabic, and I have read just about all of them. So sometimes I print out a PDF (which I must do at a copy shop) and go to Cordoba to drink coffee and read it, like a normal person anywhere else in the world. I try to go to Cordoba for my book-reading 'fix' once or twice a week, but it depends on how busy I am. There are times when I don't go for weeks due to my volunteering and university work. But I get very book-hungry when that happens.

My university has a library, but the books it holds are out of date and there are few novels by popular authors. You can hardly find a book by William Shakespeare, Charles Dickens or Agatha Christie, and novels by contemporary writers like John Green, the author of *The Fault in our Stars*, are impossible to find. The university library *does* carry a selection of books about reading and writing, and I have read all of them. For example, I love this excerpt from *Principles of Upbringing Children*, a Quran-based guide by Ayatullah Ibrahim Amini. In Chapter 72, 'The Habit of Reading Books', the author writes:

A good book always has a salutary effect on the mind of a reader. It will elevate spirit and thoughts. It will augment his store of knowledge. Books help in correcting moral ineptitude. Particularly in these days of mechanical existence, when people have hardly any time to attend meetings and symposia, the best source of acquiring religious and general knowledge are books that can be browsed whenever a person finds some time to spare. It is possible that the reading of books might have a deeper impact on the minds of the readers than other sources of acquiring knowledge.

I agree with Amini. Reading makes me feel alive. The more I read, the more I fall in love with the characters; it's like I am making new friends. When I read, I feel as though I can overcome my problems, frustrations and tendency to overthink my life.

In fact, in the summer of 2014 – during that miserable time of shelling, bombardment and death – I read day and night. It was a way for me to cope. I read on my small phone; it really hurt my eyes. I vividly remember a nightmarish evening when I was reading a book called *Peace* by science fiction writer Gene Wolfe. It is the story of a man growing up in a small Midwestern town in the early to mid-twentieth century, narrated by a character named Alden Dennis Weer. I was deeply engrossed in reading when suddenly a building nearby was hit by a ferocious rocket. The ground shook underneath my feet. I thought to myself, *I wish this Alden fellow would come and see how the hell we live here!*

Although my desire to read is often thwarted, I feed

my passion in many ways. For example, I post quotes from books I have read on Facebook. I constantly search the internet for novels by new authors. I lead book discussions at my university. I look on YouTube for videos of authors reading their work. And I search for photographs of the great libraries in the world, such as the ones in London, Washington, DC and Alexandria, Egypt. I ask myself: *Will I be lucky enough to visit these places one day? Or, because I am Gazan, will I forever be denied the pleasure of going overseas and experiencing the reality of these places?* I yearn to have a decent library in Gaza and for a good environment in which to read. Is this too much to hope?

Khaled now lives in Turkey, where he completed his master's in English language and literature in 2021. He teaches high school English and is the author of *Grief is My Second Language*. Khaled's family remain in the Gaza Strip and he hopes to someday return to them and to what remains of his home.

Friends for ever . . . we thought
by Mosab Abu Toha, mentored by Pam Bailey

The first time I lost a close friend was during the 2014 Israeli assault, when my best friend Ezzat was murdered by Israeli forces. We had been good friends since secondary school, where we studied in the same class for years. We both shared a love of reading, football and spending the summers supporting our families by working at coffee shops on the beach. For days, Ezzat and I looked for work together during the holidays, but the stress was bearable because we wandered from place to place together.

I also remember watching Barcelona football matches together, at my house. We were both huge fans of the Barcelona team. We'd visit sports shops to buy the Barcelona uniform. He bought Lionel Messi's shirt, and I bought the shirts for Zlatan Ibrahimović and Thierry Henry.

Ezzat was polite and humble. He seemed to always have a bright smile on his face. One Friday morning, I called him and we agreed to walk to the beach together. Upon reaching his house, I found him helping his neighbour, carrying buckets of sand upstairs. Ezzat's neighbour was repairing two bedrooms that had been partially damaged in the 2012 Israeli assault on Gaza.

Ezzat apologised profusely to me for having to cancel our walk to the beach. Then, he asked me to help him with the sand!

Ezzat had just completed his computer science degree at the University of Applied Sciences. He had experienced some financial difficulties that caused him to fall behind, but finally he finished his final exams. I was honoured to be invited to the discussion of his graduation project, where we took our last photo together. We hadn't seen each other much during our university years, since we attended different schools. (I went to the Islamic University of Gaza, where I studied English.) However, we stayed close friends.

The last time we were together, I invited Ezzat to join me to eat a treat made by my mother, which she prepared just for us. My mother baked a Gazan cake called bee cell (a type of pastry filled with chocolate that looks like a beehive). He came to pay me a Ramadan visit. Gazans normally exchange visits during this holy month.

The last time I heard Ezzat's voice was just after the Israeli assault on Gaza began on 8 July 2014, when he called to check on me and my family. Amid the shelling and bombing, my phone rang. It was Ezzat. We implored each other to take care of our families.

On 23 July, in the afternoon, a friend called and told me that Ezzat had been hit by a missile and killed. I was shocked. I was told that Ezzat had visited a mosque for the noon prayer. On his way home to evacuate his family, the Israeli missile hit.

At the time, I was in Gaza City, in the centre of the Strip, translating for some journalists. Ezzat and I both lived about twenty minutes away from the city, in northern Gaza. I left my colleagues and hailed a taxi. My heart pounded. I prayed that the person who had been killed was really someone else, perhaps with the same name. When I was 500 metres from our neighbourhood hospital, I saw a crowd of people carrying someone on a stretcher. It was my dearest friend Ezzat. I joined them, looking into his face: there was a hole between his eyes and deep lacerations on his neck and cheeks. I cried, simultaneously trying to wipe away the tears, to hide them from everyone else.

We took Ezzat's body to the mosque, where we said the *Janaza* prayer, which Muslims say for the dead. I kissed him goodbye, then we headed to the cemetery. I couldn't believe it was the last time I would see my friend. I hugged and shook hands with his father and brothers.

A few days later, Ezzat's family's house was badly damaged when their neighbour's home was hit. His mother went into shock. She had lost her child, and now her house was in ruins. When I went to the family's *aza'a* – a tent where people come to sympathise with relatives who have lost a loved one – Mohammad, Ezzat's brother, fainted on the stairs of their damaged house. We heard him falling and found him unconscious.

When I entered Ezzat's bedroom, I opened his wardrobe and looked at his clothes. I burst into tears.

I glanced at Ezzat's Messi shirt. His father saw me and hugged me for a while. I told him: 'I bought this T-shirt with Ezzat in 2010. He used to wear it when we played football together.' His father cried and told me: 'You can keep it for yourself.' I took the shirt and thanked him.

Before the Israeli assault, Ezzat's family had managed a bookshop that supported them. Ezzat was the clerk. There is no bookshop now because everything has been damaged. Ezzat's family now live in a flat they rent from a neighbour.

On 8 September last year, Ezzat's family invited me to attend his university graduation ceremony. When the official announced Ezzat's name, his father stepped up to receive his certificate. The audience applauded loudly. A hot tear dripped from my eye. Later that month, when I was on the stage at my own graduation ceremony, I imagined that Ezzat was clapping for me. It was a profoundly ambivalent day for me. I am sure I wasn't the only graduate to feel this way, as we struggled with memories of those we had lost while we moved forward.

Mosab escaped Gaza in December 2023 along with his wife and three children. As they left, he was detained by Israeli forces, separated from his family, stripped, beaten and interrogated for days. He was released only after an international outcry. Today, he lives in the United States. His debut book of poetry, *Things You May Find Hidden in My Ear***,**

won the Palestine Book Award and an American Book Award. It was also a finalist for the National Book Critics Circle Award and the Derek Walcott Prize for Poetry. His second book of poetry, published in October 2024, is *Forest of Noise*.

CHAPTER TWO
2016

Nightmare
by Malak Mattar, mentored by Pam Bailey

It was a nightmare.
In the morning, I opened my eyes.
It was not like any morning.
Everything around me seemed out of focus.

I thought my family were sleeping, but they were not.
I thought I had shelter, but I did not.
I thought I had friends, but I did not.
I thought I had a dream, but I did not.
I thought I had a doll, but I did not.
I thought there was a garden, but there was not.
I thought the sea was blue, but it was not.

Everything was silent like a threat, except death,
and the sound of my feet.
I ran as if there was a destination,
but death chased me and
I ran to assure myself I still lived.
I discovered a lake. It was like a blurry mirror
in which I was reflected.

I touched myself like a blind person,
and saw my face was as grey as the colour of dust

and my hair as red as the colour of blood.
The lake had shaped my face,
like war had shaped my life.

Malak left Gaza to earn her bachelor's degree from Istanbul Aydin University and launch an art career that has led to exhibitions around the world. She returned to Gaza, then left again for a creative residency in the UK just one day before the genocide broke out. Fortunately, her family have been able to evacuate to Egypt. Today, Malak is working towards a master's degree in fine art in the UK, where she wrote and illustrated *Sitti's Bird*, the story of how a little girl in Gaza finds strength and hope through painting.

Always on the inside looking out
by Enas Ghannam, mentored by Howard Kaplan

I was surfing on Facebook when I saw a photo album of a friend, who is not Palestinian. The cover picture showed him sitting in a garden on a chair swing. There were green trees and a round table in the corner, covered by a red cloth and shaded by an umbrella. It seemed like it was overlooking a sea or lake. It looked like such a charming place to be.

I know my friend travels a lot, so I wondered where he was this time. I opened the album and looked at the pictures, smiling and impressed with the beauty of the scenes. Suddenly, my eyes froze on the words 'West Bank'. I looked at the comment below: 'Having a great time in the West Bank. Behind me is Lake Tiberias.' I stopped smiling; instead, I looked at one photo after another with envy. I read the comments, but no longer smiled.

'We prayed at al-Aqsa Mosque,' he posted. 'The feeling when being in a holy land is indescribable.'

There were also photos of the Dome of the Rock, Jerusalem, Nazareth, Ashkelon, Nablus and Jericho.

My heart felt as if it would leap out of my chest – exploding in protest. Hundreds of questions crowded into my mind, but I couldn't focus on any of them. They popped and disappeared at the same time. Only one question emerged clearly: 'Why can't I go there? What or who gives him that right to go? I'm OK with not being able to visit any other country, but shouldn't I be able to visit my own at least? What gives him the right to tour the cities of my country when I can't do that?'

I couldn't help it; I cried.

I was twelve years old in the year 2000, when my father told us we would go to Jerusalem the next Friday. I was very happy and excited; it would be my first time to leave Gaza. I told my friends, who were jealous.

I imagined how it would feel to travel, riding in the car for a whole day; I day-dreamed about different scenarios: *Will we eat in the car? Maybe we will stop somewhere. I need to check that our camera is working. What will I ask Allah for when I pray at al-Aqsa Mosque? I need to prepare a list of all the things I need Him to do for me. I also need to prepare a list of things to do in Jerusalem. Will we stay there, or will we go to other places? We have relatives in Nablus I have never seen before. Will I get to see the mountains of Nablus? I have never seen a real mountain before. Will it be cold? Oh, Allah, please make it snow; I would love to see snow. Oh, dear Friday, when will you come?*

On Thursday 28 September 2000, however, former Israeli Prime Minister Ariel Sharon strode into the al-Aqsa Mosque (one of Islam's holiest sites), and the Second Intifada erupted. I never left Gaza, and I have never dared to dream again.

Eman, my closest friend, had never left Gaza

either. That somehow made the disappointment easier to handle, since misery likes company. Then she became sick and needed to go to Jerusalem for treatment. After months of working to get the Ministry of Health to certify that she needed help, and after the papers were delayed by the Israeli government for some time, she finally got permission to go. And she went.

'We are not alive in Gaza,' she told me later. She said that the moment you cross through the Erez terminal (out of Gaza and into what is now Israel), you know you are in a totally different, more 'luxurious' country, with different people and a different way of life. She prayed in the al-Aqsa Mosque and toured the malls of Jerusalem.

'It's like a country of different cultures,' she said. 'You see all kinds of people there: Japanese, Americans, Asian and Europeans.' She was like my eyes; I listened raptly to her, feeling as if I was there, yet I wasn't. She showed me the photos she took in the Church of the Holy Sepulchre.

Should I become sick so I can go there too? I thought.

When Eman and I went on a trip inside Gaza a month later, we boarded the bus and she said: 'Oh, that reminds me of the bus station in Israel.' When she was there, she had waited on a bench for the bus to come and take her. 'It doesn't wait for anyone,' she explained. 'It stops near a bench for three minutes, then it moves; it respects people's time.'

I nodded and said: 'Aha.' But ... I felt betrayed. Before, when it seemed as if everyone else had travelled and seen 'not-Gaza' places, she, like me, had not. She had been with me; but now she was with 'them'. And now I feel alone.

Enas went on to become a Gaza project manager for We Are Not Numbers, and – after leaving for a literature festival just weeks before the launch of the genocide – now lives with her aunt in the United States. Enas works as a coordinator with the United Holy Land Fund, which aids Palestinians in the Occupied Territories.

The occupation of the mind
by Aya Nashwan, mentored by Pam Bailey

I never thought my dream of pursuing education outside Gaza would turn into a curse one day. I was determined to travel abroad to study, believing it was my best chance to escape the prison that Gaza has become. I never dreamed that when the time came, I would actually turn the opportunity down.

Two years ago, I was in the last year of high school, called the *tawjihi* [the exam that must be completed at the end, and decides whether you will be accepted into college, and for what major]. I studied for long hours so I could graduate with the highest grade-point average, thus assuring I would get a scholarship to attend a university outside.

Finally, my final exams were done; vacation started and I could look forward to relaxing with my family while I waited to hear if I had been awarded a scholarship.

But those good times were not to be. A week later, I was awakened at 4 a.m. by the sound of bombs. *It could be a nightmare*, I thought to myself, and returned to sleep. However, a few minutes later, there was another explosion. I jumped out of my bed, running to my parents' room. 'The third war is starting,' I shouted.

Days of killing and destruction followed and my fear increased. Each day I wondered if it would be the last of my life. Would I become just a number in the list of deaths broadcast on the news? I asked these questions every day during the war.

Despite all of my apprehensions, however, I kept waiting for the day when the Palestinian Ministry of Education would announce the *tawjihi* ranking on TV and radio and in the newspaper.

'Aya, no one will care about your result; it is war,' Mom said, trying to ease my stress. I refused to listen. *I won't let anything destroy my hopes, even this savage war*, I thought to myself.

On 15 July, six days after the war began, the minister of education decided to announce the *tawjihi* results, despite the atmosphere of dread. At 8 a.m., I received a call from my aunt, saying, 'Congratulations! You got first place in all of Palestine.' It was an unforgettable moment, a mixture of happiness and fear. I had achieved my biggest dream. But how could I celebrate? A few minutes later, a shell landed on our neighbour's house, as if to mock me.

That war ended after fifty-one days. We should have returned to our normal life when it finally ground to a close; I should have chosen one of the scholarships I was offered because I had earned the highest ranking in the *tawjihi*. I could have chosen to attend university in Egypt, Qatar or even the United States.

But . . . when the time came, I sat alone in my room,

unable to decide what to do. I kept remembering how worried we had been about my uncle who worked for the Red Cross; his life was in constant danger as he literally dodged bombs to save people's lives. And flashing through my mind was the story on the news of a mother killed by shrapnel from a shell that hit her neighbour's house while she prepared *iftar*, the evening meal after a long day of fasting during Ramadan. Her children were now alone.

Then there was the memory of my favourite teacher, who I lost during the massacre in Shujaiya, when we were forced to flee our home at 6 a.m. — too afraid to use a car for fear of being hit by one of the warplanes swooping low overhead.

Suddenly I knew what my decision would be. I told my parents, 'I can't leave Gaza; don't even tell me about the scholarships I could take.'

The war had left me alive, but I was now afraid to face life away. What if I travelled abroad and then another war began? Could I live in peace while family members were under attack, even dying? I chose instead to attend the Islamic University of Gaza; I preferred to lose the scholarship rather than risk losing my family while I was away.

One day, months later, I read the story that Iman Abu-Aitah wrote for We Are Not Numbers. Iman had left Gaza to study in the United States before the 2014 war. 'I did not want anything to change. I thought I could put my old life on pause and come back to pick up where

I left off,' she wrote. Yet change came, in the worst of ways; Iman lost five family members, including her parents, that summer. That was my own worst fear.

Today, I know what war means and what family means. And I wonder if I can overcome all of my fears during the next two years before I graduate. Can I be brave enough to travel to the United States for my master's degree (assuming I am allowed to leave)?

I hope time is indeed the best healer.

Aya remains in Gaza. Now married, she gave birth to her first child, Kareem, in the midst of genocide, after having emergency caesarean surgery with weak anaesthesia. He is growing up in the south of Gaza, far from her house and the room that was to be his nursery. Malnutrition and disease are serious worries. 'I cannot assure him safety,' she says. 'But he will never lack for love.'

I am a girl
by Yara Jouda, mentored by Pam Bailey

I am a girl who has no dreams and maybe no future.
In a blink of an eye, I could be without hands, heart and soul.

I am a girl who lives under a roof,
which is under a sky occupied by thousands of planes full of rockets,
who is surrounded by land without anyone to work it,
because everyone is afraid of being killed by soldiers in the watchtowers,
hidden but ready to fire at any time –
without caring who they target and how their families will survive without them.

Beyond that, there is a sea that, as much as we love it,
terrifies us, because it carries huge and creepy ships that can kill us as well.
Shall I also tell you about the beautiful park turned into scarred, barren land?
Shall I tell you I would love to fly on a plane, but I am so scared of being killed by one?

Shall I tell you that I am scared to look at the sky and count the stars,
because maybe they will suddenly turn into the lights that kill? I can't even write about these things that threaten my life without fearing I will die as a result.

They took our childhood and happiness from us, and then tell us we are the terrorists. Sorry, but I don't remember raising a weapon in your face to kill you, unless you consider the games we played to be terrorism. Do you know how much we wanted and fought in those games to be the police officer who defended the poor kids and protected them from the Israeli soldiers?
What do you expect children to do, when we are still so young, but can't erase the sounds of bombs, or the pain of losing the ones we love when a rocket falls on their house and they didn't do anything to deserve such a death? And let us not forget the closing of the crossings, making it impossible to travel. Even when we can, it's as if the names on our IDs have a red line under them, just because we are Palestinian. People treat us differently; like we are all terrorists.

I am a girl who, in parts of the world where the people 'matter', would be considered too young to ask such things, much less know anything about them.

I am a girl who is forced to be an old woman at the age of fifteen.

2016

Yara left Gaza to live with her aunt and uncle and work in Saudi Arabia, then returned to marry, shortly before the genocide broke out. Fortunately, she left when the assault was just beginning. Yara is now back in Saudi Arabia, studying for her master's degree and expecting her first child. Her parents and three of her sisters remain in Gaza.

Prison is personal for Palestinians
by Salsabeel Zeineddin, mentored by Mimi Kirk

At night, when the power cuts off in my house in Gaza, my family and I sit in the living room with candles or gas lamps. We gather without internet, television or books; we talk to pass the time until we go to bed. While it's annoying that we don't have electricity, I like these moments when my mother and father tell us stories from the past.

During these gatherings, however, my father never talks about the agony he experienced in an Israeli prison, although I know he was tortured. He talks instead about the books he read and shows us the poems he wrote. Once I found a letter he sent when he was imprisoned in the Naqab Desert, where the weather was very hot during the day and cold at night. He wrote about being sick, with no medical care.

When my mother gets tired, my father cooks for us. He is a good cook. One day, he prepared a dish he used to eat in prison, a mixture of bologna, onion, tomato and egg. It tasted terrible, but he considered it delicious because it was the best meal he had in prison.

My father was jailed for two years and two months because he drew words and pictures on the streets during the First Intifada. I'll never understand why someone would get a prison sentence of two years for making graffiti!

According to the Palestinian Ministry of Detainees' and Ex-Detainees' Affairs, more than 800,000 Palestinians have been incarcerated by the Israeli government since 1967. That's 25 per cent of the Palestinian people.

My maternal uncle also lived this miserable life for twenty-four years. He was accused of leading anti-Israeli activities and sentenced to seven life terms and twenty years (!!), along with more than 750 other people during the First Intifada. Although he was jailed just six months after his wedding, his wife never asked for a divorce; she decided to wait for him because she believed the resistance would eventually end the occupation.

Every month, my grandmother, my aunts and my mother would begin preparing in the early morning on the day they planned to visit my uncle, although only two were allowed to see him each time. They would wake before dawn, cook foods he couldn't get in prison, then start the journey from Gaza to Nafha Prison near Beersheba (in Israel).

My mother recalls this journey as long and demeaning. The group spent the whole day travelling to see my uncle for only half an hour. Some days they came back to Gaza without having seen him because he was in the prison hospital or solitary confinement. As they passed through many checkpoints, Israeli soldiers used dogs to search them, which was frightening and humiliating. On some days, they spent many hours waiting in very hot or cold weather.

My grandmother was illiterate, but she always waited impatiently for mail from my uncle, delivered by his lawyer, who would read the letters to her. These letters were like a treasure to her; she never let us touch them when we were children. But I was always curious about my uncle, so I searched for the letters and read them.

My uncle expressed his love and longing for all of us and asked about each family member. Like my father, he tried not to mention the brutality he faced and instead said he was doing OK. The first letter I ever wrote was to him when I was ten years old – to a prisoner I had never met because he was jailed before I was born.

In June 2006, after Hamas captured Israeli soldier Gilad Shalit, the Israeli government barred Palestinians from Gaza from visiting their relatives in prison. After that, my family didn't see my uncle. My grandmother and grandfather died the next year, never seeing their son again.

During this period, on every Saturday at 6 p.m., my mother sat by the phone and waited for it to ring. Although my uncle was not allowed to call from prison, he would try his best to phone in secret. All of us sat around her in silence.

When I had the opportunity to talk to him, he always urged me to do well in school and promised me gifts if I got high marks. I still remember the sweet taste of the chocolate he sent me through my mother; it was delicious! I told him how much I loved and missed him, even though I had never met him face to face. He was a human, husband and beloved uncle. I was eager to meet him.

In October 2011, I was a university student, no longer the child who searched secretly for her uncle's letters. One Saturday evening, we gathered as usual in the near-dark. The phone rang. My father answered and someone said many prisoners would be freed soon – my uncle among them. On 18 October, he was released as part of the prisoner swap for Gilad Shalit.

Now it is 2016, and my uncle sometimes joins us for our shadowy evenings. He is not the same person after all those years of imprisonment; he talks very little. However, my uncle is free, and he and his wife had their first son recently. Although he was liberated, there still are more than 7,000 Palestinians held hostage in Israel's prisons, many for absurd sentences for small acts, some who have never even stood trial. No one knows when they will be free.

Now living in Qatar, Salsabeel works for a TV channel that specialises in documentaries. Her family have managed to evacuate from Gaza.

Mahmoud: a victim of bureaucracy, not war
by Said Alyacoubi, mentored by Hatim Kanaaneh

'It will be an important part of your job to deal with human tragedy with a strong heart.' This was the warning from my instructors when I first entered medical school six years ago. I asked myself, *Isn't everything I have experienced in Gaza already enough for my heart to be strong?* I never thought, however, that a tragedy might be of our own making.

I had known Mahmoud for just two weeks. I first met him during a routine, daily round with one of the paediatric consultants at the European Gaza Hospital. The five-year-old boy sat on the floor by his bed in Room 3 of the paediatric department, eating his breakfast with a smile on his face.

'He doesn't like to lie in bed,' his mother explained. 'He may be sick, but he doesn't like to be a patient.'

The next few times I saw him after that, he was either playing contentedly with his toys or talking cheerily to someone else in his room. All the staff on the floor knew Mahmoud for his simple, sunny spirit. We adored him and hoped fervently that his health would improve.

Mahmoud first became ill years before, when he suffered multiple asthmatic attacks and chest infections. Then he received a much more serious diagnosis.

'That day when Mahmoud came back from school with a swollen neck and constant cough was the worst day in my life,' his mother recalled. She brought him to the hospital and after several exams and tests, the doctor in charge delivered the devastating news: Mahmoud had a type of cancer called lymphoma, and it already was in an advanced stage – spreading throughout his body.

'There is nothing we can do here to help him,' the doctor told Mahmoud's mother. 'We will have to apply for permission to refer him out.'

Sometimes, due to shortages of medicines, absence of proper technology or lack of specific expertise caused by the Israeli blockade, our health system in Gaza is inadequate to treat certain patients, and they must be sent to the West Bank or Israel. This requires a nerve-racking delay as the families wait for the Palestinian Authority (PA) to agree to cover their treatment, a hospital to accept the patient and the Israeli government to give permission for them to pass through the Erez border crossing.

When I saw Mahmoud's mother after the decision to refer him out, she was greatly relieved. After forty-five days of waiting, the PA had finally agreed to pay the cost of Mahmoud's referral to one of the hospitals in Israel, and the hospital had agreed to admit him. Now, she had to wait again, this time for a call informing the family that Israel had given permission for Mahmoud to leave Gaza through Erez.

A week later, we passed by Mahmoud's bed again, but

he was not there. We asked the doctor in charge about him, and he replied simply: 'He died.' He had suffered an attack of severe respiratory distress and was rushed to the intensive care unit. His mother told me she felt like his eyes were pleading with her not to leave him. Half an hour later, one of the physicians told her: 'We couldn't do anything to save him.' On 5 January 2015, Mahmoud's file was closed, the final step in the referral process still pending.

Patients too frequently die while they wait for referrals to be approved. I used to believe all these failures were the responsibility of the Israeli government, since it controls and restricts the opening of our borders. And it certainly played a role in Mahmoud's death. But it was also our fault. We delayed a decision on financial coverage of his referral for more than six weeks. By then, it was already too late.

I don't know the reasons that caused the delay in a decision for Mahmoud, but whatever they were, they were not justified. Because of the delay, Mahmoud is gone. And meanwhile, others like him are still waiting.

Said is now a surgeon in training in the UK. Although most of his family have evacuated to Egypt, his sister (a WANN writer) remains in Gaza.

My life is dedicated to my dad
by Hind Khoudary, mentored by Hannah Ballard

'Hind, do you know that chairs were invented so you can sit on them, rather than on my lap?'

Dad always tried to persuade me to sit on the chair beside him instead of in his lap, and I never did. I was attached to my dad; I would even go to work with him. I was his only daughter among nine children; I was his pampered girl.

But then we were forced to be apart for a long time. Dad left Gaza in June 2007, when clashes erupted between the two political parties, Hamas and Fatah, for control of Gaza. My eight brothers, Mom and I stayed behind, and then the closed borders prevented us from seeing him for five years.

In the summer of 2012, coming up to my senior year of high school, a miracle happened. We had the opportunity to leave Gaza and join Dad in the UAE. I felt numb the moment I saw my father; I didn't believe he was in front of me. I hugged him, touched his hands, looked into his eyes. I felt so safe to be back in my dad's arms.

The UAE was heaven compared to Gaza. We had a new house, attended a new school, made new friends . . . began a new life. Unfortunately, we had to live in a city other than where Dad worked, to keep costs down. We only saw Dad on weekends, and I never got enough of him.

Then everything changed again on Friday 28 December. The whole family were gathered in front of the TV drinking tea. Suddenly, Dad stood up, coughed and fell to the floor. I remember how his eyes rolled and his face turned red. How my mom froze, crying and staring at my dad. How my brothers and I screamed: 'Dad. Dad!'

Suddenly, he opened his eyes. He stood up, denied he wasn't well. He got ready to go back to his city, taking his laundry and food for the week. He hugged me tight. I had a feeling this was our last hug; I could feel my heart breaking into pieces. He whispered: 'Take good care of yourself, my darling. I'll always be proud of you.' I didn't understand why he said this.

I didn't sleep that night. I cried the whole night and fell asleep at 7.30 a.m.

Mom woke me at 11 that morning: 'Hind, your dad isn't answering his phone. Hind, your dad never does this.' At that moment, I was sure my dad was no longer alive.

Seven hours later, we received the news. Dad had passed away from a sudden heart attack. 29 December 2012 was the darkest day of my life. I lost my father, I lost my strength, I lost my life.

I never imagined myself carrying on without him, but I couldn't shed a tear. My brothers and Mom were in shock. Mom cried, while my brothers didn't talk. I updated

Facebook to let the rest of our family in Gaza know. Everyone started to call; they couldn't believe my father had died. Our uncles said we had to come back to Gaza.

We knew we were going back to a form of hell. Back to the blockade and twelve-hour electricity cuts. Back to a place where we might die any second. We had no other choice; we had to give up our life there and move back to Gaza.

I had always dreamt of being a TV broadcaster or a correspondent for the BBC, but I sacrificed my dreams to stay with my mom in Gaza. I knew I helped her be strong. I received a scholarship to study business administration at the Islamic University of Gaza and began attending school.

It was my dad's dream to see me successful. He wanted me to be a strong girl who nothing could break. When Dad passed away, he took my dreams with him. But now I'm working hard to make them happen, to make him proud of me. I'll confront all challenges and I'll become the person I know I can be.

In the four years since Dad's death, I've become a very resilient person. I guess I saw the dark side of life and I wanted to bring back the light. I started working on the things I'm passionate about. I joined a volunteering team that helps people all around Gaza, including distributing wheelchairs to disabled children. I started taking courses to become a TV correspondent. I want to show the truth we are living to the world, and that's why I joined We Are Not Numbers.

Strength comes from hardship. You might think you can't make your dreams come true, but nothing can truly break you. I've stopped dreaming of leaving Gaza, because I'm sure one day I can help make this place better. Despite the difficulties we face daily, I won't give up on my country. I'll spread the message of love, strength, hope and tolerance for which my country stands.

Destiny takes you to a path you can't know. Please, my destiny, allow my dreams to come true.

Hind's dream came true. Today, she is a prominent journalist in Gaza, covering the genocide for media such as Al Jazeera English and Anadolu Agency. In July 2024, Hind reported on the killing of Ismail Alghoul by Israeli forces for an Al Jazeera broadcast. She was visibly upset as she spoke about the dangers facing journalists in Gaza: 'We do everything [to stay safe]. We wear our press jackets. We wear our helmets. We try not to go anywhere that is not safe. [. . .] But we have been targeted in normal places where normal citizens are. [. . .] at the same time, we want to report, we want to tell the world what's going on.'

Love letter to Gaza
by Nada Hammad, mentored by Tom Sperlinger

Every time I say I want to travel and see the world, my mom and dad lecture me about how they've been to every other place in the world, and Gaza is the greatest. Deep down, I realise they are right for the most part, but someone with my imagination doesn't want to spend her life in one place. I want to see the world and try new experiences. I want to visit England during winter and build a snowman. I want to spend at least a year in Scotland among all the green fields. I want to go to the 'wild west' of America, or to the south and try to pick up the accent. My bucket list is bottomless. I want to go everywhere and experience everything I've never had a chance to do here in Gaza.

I live in a small part of Jabalia camp called Tel al-Zataar in the north of Gaza. Our area is where most of the action takes place during Israeli aggressions. Our camp is the second closest to Beit Hanoun, the town right on the border with Israel. We are one of the first areas to be bombed in any attempt to secure the northern part of Gaza when a land invasion is planned. There is an empty piece of land a stone's throw away from my house, a square patch with a few scattered olive trees, and it was hit at least a dozen times in each of the past three wars. Sometimes, it feels like I can hear the echo of the bombing when I walk past.

I have lived through three wars, about a dozen invasions and nine years of siege. I also have waited through God knows how many hours for the electricity to come back on so I can finally get online, or iron tomorrow's outfit and hijab, or watch the TV show I'm waiting for. Despite it all, I still love it.

When I think about it closely, I think I have a love/hate relationship with Gaza. I hate the fact that I am trapped here more than anything. I hate how even though Gaza has given me nothing but heartache and pain – destroyed homes, dead loved ones, homeless people every direction I look – I still can see a flowering bush pulsing with colour next to the ruins of someone's home, or remember a childhood adventure with my dad in one of the old bookshops. Then I fall in love with this place all over again. It's what Mahmoud Darwish [the most famous Palestinian poet] expressed when he said: *We have on this land that which makes life worth living.**

I love the sense of togetherness in Gaza. Despite the hardships, people still care for each other. During the last war, which Israel dubbed Operation Protective Edge, more than 96,000 houses were destroyed either fully or partially, and more than half a million Gazans were left with no shelter over their heads. During these

---

* *'On This Land'* by Mahmoud Darwish.

hard times, some people cleared their basements or roofs for others to use. When relatives' houses were damaged, many people took them into their homes and split the space, food, clothes and everything else.

I love how we manage to find a way to cope with every obstacle, despite the seeming impossibility. A few years ago, when I was still in high school, we visited my aunt's house when the electricity shortage was at its peak. The fuel supply was so low that we went without electricity for at least sixteen hours a day, if not more. When it got dark and there was still no light, my Uncle Jamal hooked up a couple of low-voltage light bulbs to his car battery and lit the house up. Everyone cheered.

I love how everyone in Gaza is a sea person (except our mothers, probably because they don't like rinsing sand out of our clothes). Sometimes during the hot summer days, it seems as if the entire city is out on the beach. One time, my dad had promised us a trip to the sea. It was July, the hottest summer month, and all of us needed to cool off. It took us maybe two hours of grovelling and promising to behave and get as little sand as possible on our bodies and clothes before Mom agreed to come with us. When we got there, the beach was packed with people. You'd think only the kids and their obliging parents would be there, but that wasn't the case. It seemed as if all of Gaza City was there – old people sitting under umbrellas; young men playing water football or volleyball; kids building sandcastles, or at least attempting to; older youths burying each other in the sand after spending ages digging big holes to do so. We swam, we ate watermelon, and we laughed.

I love our bumpy roads, and how I might be walking leisurely one minute and jumping over holes the next. I love the uneven streets because of the many memories I've made with my friends on these roads. We walk them on our way to eat ice cream, arguing over everything from the flavour we want to try this time, to who's godmothering whose (future) baby since she has a better sense of fashion. (Hint: I have a better sense of fashion.)

I love the fact that you can stargaze to your heart's content because most areas don't have electricity much of the time.

I love Gaza for its people, especially my family and friends. I love it for the way I am accepted for my brain; nerds and bookworms are celebrated here, unlike many other societies. My time in high school, for example, wasn't a popularity contest. I went to an all-girls school. All of us wore the same uniform, although there were slight differences in this girl's sneakers or that one's backpack. What mattered wasn't the outside appearance – and boy, did I look like a potato back in the day! Instead, we competed for who read the most books and who could figure out this maths problem or the answer to that physics question. It was an academic contest, not a fashion one. I must admit it did get stressful sometimes, to always try to be better and do more. However, it was rewarding. I loved being among the best students in my class. It was a satisfaction unlike anything else.

2016

I love the good, the bad, the heartbreaking and everything in between because I don't think I would be the person I am today if I hadn't lived in Gaza.

In one of his many *Letters to Melina*, Franz Kafka writes: *Now I'm even losing my name – it was getting shorter and shorter all the time and is now: Yours.* I am no Franz Kafka and Gaza is no Melina but I still love Gaza enough to send a letter to her with a declaration of belonging.

CHAPTER THREE

2017

Gazapore
by Omnia Ghassan, mentored by Kevin Hadduck

Author's note: One day my mama said: 'You know, Omnia? There is so much passion here in Gaza, so much talent that needs to be discovered. If all of our unemployed graduates could use their skills to revive the Gaza Strip, it could be more developed than Singapore. But the siege is preventing us from capitalising on this potential!' So I started to imagine Gaza becoming like Singapore...

My beautiful city with skyscrapers,
depot, seaport, airport.
My Gazapore is famous for
its citruses, olives and *kenafa*,
which I eat every single day.
My hunger can't be silenced
without their juice
flowing through me.
I'm Gazaporean.

These things run through my veins
instead of my blood!
And oh! The mountains,
green orchards and clear sea.
I can travel outside, but I want to stay.

I have so many pictures of cities
I want to visit, but I don't want to leave.
Rome, Barcelona, London and New York
are all waiting for me to set foot in them.
No! Gazapore is my homeland, my city
and my refuge. How can I leave?
Do I not have all I need?

My imagination has run wild.
I've forgotten that Gaza is no Singapore,
no city open to the world!

We are trapped on four sides!
I lack everything: work, electricity,
water, security . . . and freedom.
I can't even see past Erez or the Rafah gates.
Yet my enemies go wherever they like.

I can't call my country my own,
while my enemies rename every place in it.
Areeha's citruses wait to be peeled and juiced.
Nasra's olives are ripe enough to be picked.
Nablus' *kenafa* is ready to be tasted.

Al-Jaleel Mountains wait for my footsteps.
Haifa's green orchard greets me.
The Dome of the Rock shines in the sun
and is calling for me.
Where am I, in all of this?

Ah! What's gotten into me today?
I shouldn't think that way!
I've no right to raise my voice.
I've no right to defend my country.
I've no right to dream.
Oh, I've no right to live!

I'm Gazaporean.
That is all.

Omnia recently wrote a novel, called *Toyor Yanayer* (Birds of January), which touches on loss and trauma, and people's varied responses to tragedy. She hopes to translate it into English soon. Omnia continues to live in Gaza, reflecting: 'I look at my pictures from a year ago. They feel like they're from a different life. A different dimension. A parallel universe where I'm still me. My niece stands next to me; she looks at the pictures. "It's you," she says. Is it? Is it really me? How can she recognise me when I can't even recognise myself? When I don't even recognise my own reflection. Who am I? The person in the pictures or the one in the mirror? My friend texts me: "I miss you." *I miss me too*, I murmur.'

I want the world to know
by Anas Jnena, mentored by Pam Bailey

I want the world to know that Gaza is all about life – just like any other place in the world.

I want the world to know that Gaza is not the devastated, dusty, mouldy place too often shown on the news. I want the world to know that Palestinians are neither victims nor heroes. Just like any other people, we wake up every day to go to school or work, we laugh when we hear a funny joke and cry when we have a toothache. We love the smell of the sea and the colours of the sky, especially at sunset, and we hate seeing the dentist even when we know we should.

I want the world to know that when a Palestinian mother ululates over her son's death, it doesn't mean she's celebrating; rather, it's an often unsuccessful attempt to persuade herself and her other children that she will not let the grief engulf her, and she won't give up. But for the truth, look into her eyes and see what they speak; or, if you have enough guts, stand at her window at night to hear her moans and sighs.

I want the world to know that when Palestinian kids throw stones at Israeli soldiers sent to enforce the occupation, it doesn't mean we teach our children hatred or that we advocate violence. Rather, it's our only way of showing that we will resist and defend ourselves, that we aren't defeatists. Instead of questioning Palestinians' intentions, critics first should look for what Israel has contributed to achieving peace and justice. Expanding settlements, a decades-old siege, closed borders, scant hours of electricity a day, four wars?

I also want the world to know that despite all this, there's nothing that can stop us from falling in love . . . that we play Adam Lambert's 'Another Lonely Night' when we get dumped . . . Justin Timberlake's 'What Goes Around Comes Back Around' when we are cheated on . . . and Adele's 'Hello' when we sorely miss somebody. I want the world to know that some teens in Gaza skip their fifth class at school so they can see the girls they love and hand them naively written love letters.

I want the world to know that Palestine has writers, artists, thinkers and, most importantly, lovers. I want the world to know that we are humans just like you.

Why jello doesn't taste good any more
by Ahmed Alnaouq, mentored by Les Filotas

Most people don't visit graveyards frequently. When you do visit, you find a few people scattered around, everyone there for a different reason: a mom still mourning for her son; an orphan lying beside her parents' graves with a single flower and a tear in her eye; a widow holding her son's hand and sitting near her martyred husband's grave, updating him on her mother-in-law's injustice; an old man watering the plants on his wife's resting place.

Their reasons for being there may be different, but one thing is common – all of them visit during daylight hours. That is, except for me and my four best friends – Ahmed, Ayman (my older brother), Belal and Abdullah. We never went there during the day. We went only after midnight.

Our favourite time for a cemetery visit was a moonless night, with stray dogs barking in the streets and a light rain falling in the early winter. Does that sound creepy? We were distressed about losing our friend, Mahmoud, who was killed in 2008 by Israeli soldiers. We found serenity by sitting around his gravestone. Although he was dead, we felt Mahmoud's spirit looming over us. We found some rocks to use as seats, sat close to each other and shared our secrets.

What I loved most about these visits is that they were spontaneous; we decided on the spot and then walked. When we arrived, we gathered around his grave and recited a prayer for Mahmoud.

Time passed and our habit persisted. Mahmoud's tomb wasn't our only destination; we also visited the markers for other relatives and friends. One night, the five of us gathered around an open grave that had been prepared for a burial the next morning.

Ahmed turned to me and said: 'You don't dare get down in there, do you?' 'Why not? I surely can do it,' I replied instantly. 'I bet you won't,' Ahmed challenged me. 'Well, I will show you,' I assured him. They stripped me of any source of light, took away my mobile phone and said: 'Go ahead.' Impulsively, I climbed down into the open grave and lay down.

In Gaza, grave pits are typically lined with stones. Boards are then laid over the top, which are covered with more stones. My four friends covered the grave, preventing any source of light or fresh air from reaching me. It was after midnight on one of those hot July nights, and I felt no fear whatsoever. I was thrilled to be calmly experiencing something that many would think terrifying. I remained in the covered grave for about ten minutes. During this time, my friends pretended to leave in an attempt to frighten me. They were disappointed;

I was not frightened. When they discovered I was not going to plead with them to let me out, they opened the grave and congratulated me. 'You win.'

Two years after the graveyard incident, in 2014, Israel launched Operation Protective Edge, a brutal assault on Gaza that left more than 2,500 people dead, 13,000 injured and more than half a million displaced. Ayman, Belal and I spent all our time together. Our favourite food was jello with fruit and cream. My family knew that whenever my friends and I were together, we could be found around a bowl of jello. Even in the most dangerous times during the war, with drones hovering overhead, missiles firing and explosions everywhere, we enjoyed our jello.

Two days after our most recent bowl of jello, I received shocking news. My friends and my brother had been hit by an F-16 missile. Ayman, Ahmed and Abdullah were killed instantly, their bodies mutilated. Belal simply disappeared. I couldn't stop thinking about Belal and his mysterious disappearance. We all knew Belal had been with the others, but the ambulance crew didn't find him. The first day passed without any news about him. Eight days passed, and Belal still had not been found. Every night during that too-long week, I dreamt of Belal. Sometimes I dreamt he was alive, sometimes that he was dead and sometimes that he was wounded.

Finally, Belal's remains were found – buried two metres under the dirt. During a pause in Israel's assault on Gaza, a group of neighbours and ambulance crews dug deep into the ground and found his decomposed body in the ruins of the house where they had all been together. That day I shed no tears; I was too numb.

Three years ago, going to the graveyard had been our routine. I haven't visited there since my four best friends were killed. And I will never enjoy jello again.

A sweet spot in Gaza
by Khaled Alostath, mentored by Catherine Baker

I was walking down the street one day, going home from university, when I noticed a tiny café huddled among the huge buildings of Gaza City. 'Honey Bee' read the sign above the door. The name was repeated on a large blue-and-yellow mural that was the café's storefront. All the outdoor tables were wet and empty.

Once inside, I realised the café was nearly full. A young man with a skelctal look was sitting by the window with a beautiful young woman; they held hands while watching the rain. Some businessmen sat at another table and a few students were gathered on stools by the counter. The place was filled with tobacco smoke, the sound of conversation and speakers playing eclectic music – Bob Marley's 'Is This Love', Engelbert Humperdinck's 'How I Love You' and some strange, electronic music.

The place was hip looking. Red accents were everywhere – on the chairs, tables, ceiling ornaments and napkins. The walls were plastered with pages from Turkish and American newspapers, a mural depicting the Simpsons (*The Last Supper*) and a big sheet of black-and-white cartoon drawings. Another mural of a tree adorned the ceiling. But what really drew my attention was the glass case holding an assortment of mouth-watering desserts.

I sat at an empty table, ordered coffee and stared into its depths, deep in thought. *This is a good time to be alone, like being on a date with myself, and take a virtual trip to America by having a cinnamon roll*, I thought. To me, that plump pastry, sitting in the glass case, symbolised the place I visit in my dreams.

The waiter came by and pointed to my still-full cup of coffee. 'Here's the menu. I wonder if you don't like the coffee you ordered. I can change it for you, sir.'

'It's all great,' I reassured him.

I looked at the menu. What to choose? American (brownie, chocolate-drizzled waffle, cookie, layer cake), French (*blancmange*, *pain perdu*) or Italian (*panna cotta*)? Or how about Middle Eastern (*knafah* or pumpkin with honey)?

I heard a thick male voice, speaking in French, at the table behind me. As he stood up and passed me, he repeated: '*Une vie sans bonbons ne vaut pas la peine d'être vécue.*'

'Sorry, I don't speak French. But I'm good in English,' I said.

'A life without sweets is not much worth living,' he said, in English this time.

The couple in love laughed. I could see through the open door that the rain outside was coming down harder. The Frenchman typed something into his phone as a cigarette dangled from the corner of his mouth.

'You must be a reader,' I said, offering him a chair at my table.

'Why should I be?'

'Because that was a quote from a book, not your own words.'

'What is the name of the book? Since you think they are not my own words.'

'*Coinman: An Untold Conspiracy*, by an Indian writer named Pawan Mishra.'

'Wow! This is unbelievable. God!'

We conversed in English about books and writing. I learned the man had lived in France as a child. His loud voice and excitement made the owner come by our table, to see whether everything was OK. We assured him it was, and I ordered my cinnamon roll. The Frenchman left and then the café's owner brought my dessert.

'This is awesome,' I said to him.

'Does it taste good?' he asked, but he was confident of my answer.

'Indeed, it does,' I replied.

'Eating here won't cost you an arm and a leg, at least compared with other cafés,' he said, proudly. I asked him to sit down with me and tell me the story of Honey Bee.

Amr Sobh is the owner of this small café. He studied tourism and hospitality in Egypt and worked as a pastry chef there for a long time. When he returned to Gaza, he decided to put his learning and experience to use by creating a cultural-musical café. In 2016, Amr's dream came true.

'I was not able to think of a name in the beginning,' he said. 'So, I asked some friends and they suggested many good names, among them Honey Bee.'

My brain travelled once again to the United States. *I bet there is more than one Honey Bee café over there*, I thought to myself.

Amr was still talking. 'The main reason for the Western desserts is because no one can make them here like I do. Some cafés pretend they can make all the Western desserts, but that's not true. I know how, based on my experience baking for foreigners in Egyptian hotels.'

He added: 'Being honest is the very core of the work.'

Although Honey Bee is thriving, Amr has bigger goals. He wants to expand the café so he can welcome more guests. But he's in a struggle with the municipality in Gaza to add more outdoor tables. And he would like to expand the inside, too.

Amr stood up. 'Good food, fresh water, an occasional sweet and someone to care for,' he said. 'That's what everyone should have. A simplistic and unrealistic view I know, but it soothes me to think about it.'

'You have read Maria Snyder's *Magic Study*,' I replied, standing up to leave myself.

'No, I didn't get that out of any book. It was written on a menu in Egypt.'

Before I left, Amr asked me to write a secret message on a doily. That's when I noticed the pile of message-laden doilies on a plate on the counter. 'Life is too short; eat desserts first,' I wrote.

Ahead of me, the couple were leaving the café, still holding hands. It was thundering and the rain was torrential. As I departed, I waved to Amr with a promise to come back again.

I opened my umbrella, headphones in my ears, and walked with a feeling of peace. 'That was a really great experience,' I told myself. 'This time Honey Bee in Gaza, next time Honey Bee in the United States. Why not?'

English in context
by Haya Abdullah Ahmed, mentored by Nicholas Sherwood

English is one of the most acquired, needed and used languages in the world. No matter what your field of study, English seems to be required. If Palestinians in Gaza long for a scholarship to study abroad or to explore the world, we need to be good at English.

In conversation classes, we are asked to answer all sorts of questions in English. Once my teacher in an Amideast class asked us to describe in English what we did during our Eid holiday (a multi-day affair). I decided to have some fun and answered this way: 'On the first day, my aunts Hoyam and Sohair and my cousins visited. On the second day, we visited my grandmother and met Hoyam, Sohair and my cousins again. On the third day, we went to Sohair's home and met both Hoyam and my cousins. On the fourth day, we went to Hoyam's home and met Sohair and my cousins.' In other words: the entire holiday was like a game of musical chairs! (We call it *karasy*.) Everyone broke into laughter.

However, the textbooks we must use in class to learn conversation give us practice exercises that are equally funny, to a Gazan at least. The funniest are the exercises related to travel, since most of us are not allowed out of Gaza by the two countries that control our borders: Egypt and Israel.

Below are a few of the questions asked in these exercises, and my answers in class recently.

Q: Where will you stay during your coming holiday?

A: I will stay in my home, or in my grandmother's, aunts', uncles' or friends' homes. And I will spend my days in Gaza City's Mazaj restaurant – the same as every other 'holiday'.

Q: Do you like to travel to Canada like Jack, or like Mary to Paris?

A: Yes, but that's possible only in my dreams. Those countries won't even give me a visa, and even if they would, I'd probably have to pay a bribe of thousands of dollars to the Egyptian guards on one of the rare days the Rafah crossing is open to get out. And the Erez crossing into Israel? I could apply for a permit, but I'd probably never get an answer – which is as good as a 'no'.

Q: What is your favourite hotel?

A: [At this point, I am getting frustrated and even outraged, so I decide to fake it.] Frankly, it's difficult to choose [a chorus of giggles]. However, I'll go with the Fontainebleau Hotel.

I asked my classmates what they thought about stock questions such as these. My friend Ghada said: 'Such questions always peeve me and make me feel inferior for not being able to go beyond the borders of Gaza and not being able to go on different flavoured holidays.'

Another friend, Shaimaa, differed: 'That's true, but questions like these should still be asked to give us at least an idea of what our lives should be like. Thinking of being like Mary gives me a deep feeling of tranquillity and hope.'

Sometimes I feel like Ghada. I wish I could shout at whoever wrote these textbooks: 'For God's sake, don't mock us!' Other times, I feel like Shaimaa, thinking these questions are a source of inspiration and imagination, like a novel. I imagine myself playing and running with Anne and Diana while reading L.M. Montgomery's *Anne of Green Gables*. I imagine myself having cinnamon rolls in a Fika espresso bar and delivering my first presentation about literary translation at the University of Massachusetts. (I saw a picture of the Fika bar one time in a book, and it delivers cinnamon rolls. So fabulous!)

Stephen Hawking defines intelligence as 'the ability to adapt to change'. I believe in that. However, the ability to adapt must not mean the passive acceptance of poor circumstances or to ignore our dreams of the life we wish to live. Being too accepting will lead us to achieve nothing. I want to appreciate my life for its sweet, simple blessings: reading, writing, reciting poems, telling stories, cooking, selling falafel, singing and teaching.

But I will never forget my dreams. Someday, my dreams will come true.

Today, Haya lives in Turkey with her husband and works as an English–Arabic translator and copywriter. However, her entire family remain in Gaza, and many members of her aunt's family have been killed.

The betrayal of Wonder Woman
by Omnia Ghassan, mentored by Pam Bailey

Batman, Spider-Man, the Phantom, the Hulk: these superheroes were part of my childhood. I grew up reading comic books and watching cartoons that revolved around them. I liked them all, but the fact that the main characters were all men annoyed me. I wanted a female superhero to admire.

Then I was introduced to Diana Prince, aka Wonder Woman. She is a passionate warrior with a compassionate heart who courageously uses her strength to help those in need. In 2013, it was announced that Wonder Woman would be featured in *Batman v Superman: Dawn of Justice*. I was thrilled, until the director, Zack Snyder, revealed the actress who would play Wonder Woman: Gal Gadot, a former combat trainer for the Israeli occupation forces. (Two years later, in 2015, Gal/Wonder Woman was given her own solo movie.) Although I was thrilled for Wonder Woman, I was appalled by her avatar: Gal Gadot represented everything Wonder Woman fights *against*.

Snyder said he chose Gadot because her fierce yet kind personality fitted the role. Yet she had demonstrated she *didn't* live up to this description. Gadot served for two years in the Israeli military, training combat fighters. In 2014, those troops went to war against my land and my people. She uploaded a photo on to Instagram of herself praying with her daughter with the caption: 'I am sending my love and prayers to my fellow Israeli citizens. Especially to all the boys and girls who are risking their lives protecting my country against the horrific acts conducted by Hamas, which is hiding like cowards behind women and children.'

What Gadot didn't highlight is that the Israeli army kills Palestinian women and children. According to statistics collected by the Euro-Mediterranean Human Rights Monitor, 732 Gazan women and children were killed in Israel's 2014 offensive, and another 5,404 were injured. A third of this horrific number are permanently disabled. (Note that only 16 per cent of those killed were Palestinian resistance fighters, the ones Gadot claimed her army targeted.) In addition, according to an investigation conducted by Euro-Med, captured Palestinians were used as 'shields' by Israeli soldiers for hours at a time.

On the Israeli side, one woman and one child were killed, and none were injured. Of course, all deaths and injuries are tragic, but these numbers reveal the severe disparity in power and violence between the Palestinians and Israelis. Yet the character Gadot was playing (Wonder Woman) believes a war should be fought between equal forces, and that women and children should be protected.

It's also important to keep in mind why Palestinians resist in the first place: in Gaza, the entry and exit of all people and goods are tightly restricted. In fact, most exports are prohibited, making a healthy economy impossible and creating an unemployment rate that is the highest in the world. At the same time, we are not allowed to import most construction materials and many vital medicines. I could go on and on.

Almost six months after its release date, I finally watched the *Wonder Woman* movie. (We don't have theatres in Gaza; instead, we have to wait until movies are available online.) It was a well-done film, but casting Gadot as Wonder Woman – panicking over the well-being of women and children injured or under attack and using all her might to save them – was hypocritical. I couldn't watch with enthusiasm.

While Gadot has received a pass from Hollywood for her combative actions and rhetoric, other actors who have stood up for Palestine have been subjected to intense backlash. In 2014, actress Penelope Cruz and her husband Javier Bardem signed an open letter against 'the genocide perpetrated by the Israeli occupation army'. In response, some Hollywood executives pledged never to work with the Spanish couple. They were blacklisted for simply saying that 'Gaza is living through horror . . . while the international community does nothing.'

As a Gazan girl, I believe it is a betrayal for Wonder Woman, a symbol of peace and justice, to be played by a woman who defended Israeli forces' murder of civilians. Little girls everywhere look up to characters like Wonder Woman. What message are we sending to the next generation of female leaders?

CHAPTER FOUR
2018

How much should we risk for freedom?
by Haneen Sabbah, mentored by Mohammed Massoud Morsi

I see empty lands in front of me.
I see my dreams dance away from me.
A voice inside says: 'Go to these dreams!
Just go to that space!'
Another voice shouts: 'What if you get shot?'
The other voice responds: 'So what, at least you tried.
You tried to break the silence and the chains.
Maybe you will feel better if you die fighting for your dreams.'

But hold on.
I don't want to let go.
I don't want to lose my life.
I have so many dreams.
I have so many things I wish to do.
I have . . .
OK, I give up . . .
I don't have anything to lose.
I want to go where I belong:
Home.

I imagine a hand extending from that far-away land.
I will just take that hand

And go home.
Still . . . how will anyone hear me then?
Who will read my words?
I will be shot for trying to reach for my dreams.
I want the world to hear my reasons for marching.
We want to have a normal life with happy moments.
We want to breathe and have other worries,
besides what we will eat for the day.
We must be heard.
We must be free.

Haneen writes in this poem of the Great Return March, a weekly protest that started in 2019. Participants dreamed of being able to return to their ancestral homeland, but it soon turned deadly as they clashed with Israeli soldiers.

Haneen left Gaza well before the genocide began, courageously travelling alone to Portugal to teach, hoping that she would later be able to bring her husband and children to join her. She accomplished that goal, and now works there to elevate the Palestinian story through food and other cultural traditions. Three of her sisters and her parents remain in Gaza.

When the sea becomes a lake: the prison that is Gaza
by Ali Abusheikh, mentored by Pam Bailey

From time to time, I head to the Gaza sea, where I can breathe some fresh air and have a little chat with the blue expanse. We talk in a silent language that nobody understands but me and the sea. Whenever I go there, I usually take my little tea thermos and my phone, so I can play music.

The music of the sea is soft when the waves are calm, and so I play my own, sad and relaxing tunes – often Arabic or Turkish Sufi songs. I love to listen to Sufi music because it takes me to another, spiritual world where I find peace and tranquillity.

Sometimes I go to the sea with friends, but most frequently I go alone. The sea is my soulmate and the place where I release my stress, share my dreams and even weep freely. I sit with my back to the land, on a rock opposite the beautiful Bridge of Ashdod, where I can see the lights that so rarely glimmer in my city. I don't want to see the mourning that is ever-present in Gaza: the dim lights, dingy buildings and faces with smiles that don't reach their eyes or hearts. We are all somewhat dead inside.

At the sea, I try to convince myself that I am not

in Gaza, but somewhere else on the Mediterranean – maybe in Mykonos, Greece. I always dream big.

I feel fortunate that my house is just a short walk from the beach, but sometimes I go further to the Gaza port (al-Mina). People refer to it as a port, but it is not a real port any more. Prior to World War I, it was busy and thriving. But then the Ottoman era ended and, later, Israel imposed its blockade on Gaza (now reinforced by Egypt). Visitors see a few rusty, archaic ships from the earlier days, but the only boats that sail in those waters are those of fishermen who are allowed to go just six miles out. Still, the sea was my escape, an oasis of beauty.

But one day I realised that it, too, has its limits.

I had headed to al-Mina with two of my friends. Once we found a spot with a good view, we sat and stared at the beauty of the sea before us. The glassy surface was very calm and a deep blue. But for some reason, and for the first time, the water before me looked very confined, deeply unsettling me. I felt as if I was viewing a lake, not a sea. I knew the sea is not open to the outside world. For all practical purposes, it ends where the Israeli warships lurk, ready to shoot at any boat that attempts to go out too far or even to sail in to visit us.

Even the tranquil blue of its water is deceiving – mixed as it is with the blood of Palestinian fishermen and those brave international activists who died at the hands of the Israelis in their attempt to visit Gaza. And then there are the toxic pollutants that pour into it every day because the blockade makes it impossible to have a functioning waste-treatment system.

My friends were chit-chatting, but my thoughts drowned them out. I imagined where those waters could take me if only I could sail freely. Going north was Turkey or Cyprus, travelling west would lead me to Tunisia, Italy or even Spain, and to the south is Egypt. But then an insidious, sarcastic voice in my head interrupted. It said: *This so-called sea will take you nowhere. You can go nowhere, Ali! Have you lost your mind? Look around. This is not even a sea; it's a lake. It's a three- to six-mile lake, with its limits changing at Israel's whim. It never gets wider, just narrower.*

When I turned away from the sea to look at my home, Gaza City, I asked in confusion: *What has happened? Why does your sea feel and look like a lake?* Gaza replied: *It was a sea, Ali. It was, but not any more.*

I wasn't shocked by the city's answer, although I had long been deceived by its spectacular view. Yes, Gaza looks beautiful, especially in photos, but its beauty is fake – often helped by the inventive filters used by photographers. Gaza seems strong and steadfast in photos, but in reality it is so very vulnerable. The lack of fresh water, of medicine, of electricity, of jobs that pay sustainable salaries, of construction materials, of good-quality goods, of *life*, is eating away at its soul, our souls. Gaza is at death's door.

Then I glimpsed a group of seagulls flying over the

fishermen's small, dusty boats. The existence of seagulls proved it is still a sea in its 'heart' – although their calls sounded like screaming, as if pleading for help. It's like they are imprisoned just as Gazans are, even though they have wings and can travel, unlike us. We all want to be free like seagulls are, travelling whenever and wherever, without the need for a permit.

Ali travelled to Qatar to pursue a master's degree in digital humanities and social sciences. In 2022, after he graduated, he returned to Gaza – and was caught in the genocide that broke out in October 2023. Just before the border closed in summer 2024, Ali managed to return to Qatar. He is working in communications and hopes to bring his mother out of Gaza.

New girl on the block
by Iman Inshasi, mentored by Deborah Root

A normal flight from the UAE to Cairo, Egypt, takes about five hours. But when measured by the impact on my life, the distance seemed a lot further. Despite my long obsession with observing clouds and photographing them as they caress the Sun, I hated them as I stared out of the plane window. Why didn't they release a shower of rain, snow or even gigantic hail, forcing the plane to make an emergency landing? Flight attendants came and went like bees, but I felt like I was chained to my seat – like a hostage waiting for salvation. I used to think of flight as the path to freedom and independence, but not any more.

My swollen eyes couldn't bear the sight of the calm sky and I soon closed all of the window blinds. Tears ran down my cheeks like a river. A blanket covered my body and when a hospital-like breakfast tray was laid on the fold-down table in front of me, I felt like an invalid. I was only fifteen, yet I felt like my life was coming to an end. 'Who leaves the UAE to go to Gaza?'

I won't deny hating Gaza even before I arrived, and I vividly recall praying to God for some kind of miracle that would mean we had to return to Abu Dhabi. But once I saw my dad carrying our bags when we landed in Cairo, a bad word that starts with an F leapt to my tongue. I knew there was no going back.

I naively asked Mum: 'So what now?' She replied with what was left of her energy. 'We take a taxi, then another taxi, then another taxi.' (Israel doesn't permit Gaza to have its own airport, so we must enter through Egypt.) And that's what we did – crammed in like sardines. I snapped at Mum: 'Did you bring the entire house from UAE to here? We can't even move in this car.'

During the almost eight-hour ride, I existed in what I remember as a 'half' phase: half asleep, half hungry, half crying. It was so oppressively hot I felt like dry toast. I finally did fall asleep, though, without even realising it. Then Mum was shaking me like a sack of potatoes, saying: 'We're home.'

A stranger snatched my handbag. We stared at each other for fifteen endless seconds, the longest eye contact I've ever made with someone I don't know. 'Welcome home,' the robber finally said, looking at me from head to toe. I grimaced at his greeting; this was not my home.

The 'robber' was actually my cousin and he, along with some other men, welcomed us to the house where I'd have to live.

When I entered the living room, I felt like I had walked in on the meeting of a support group. Chairs were organised in a C shape, with seven young men sitting in them. (I soon learned that family gatherings are a must in this culture; I had never realised my family was this big!) I faked a smile and sat for four hours, answering what seemed to me to be highly intrusive questions. I finally decided to call it a day when one of my cousins said for the umpteenth time: 'You're not going back, you know.'

My life-changing flight and the endless taxi ride meant I needed a life-changing shower. Burdened with exhaustion and grief, I grabbed a towel and my favourite pyjamas and escaped into a dull, grey bathroom. The floor was bare concrete, without a mirror, bathtub or towel rods. I didn't sign up for this! I turned on the shower spigot and waited for the water to cleanse away my mood of foreboding. Instead, I tasted grit in my mouth. 'Yes, the water in Gaza isn't clean,' my uncle shouted in response to my yell of 'there's sand in the water!'.

It took me five minutes to progress through each phase of grief: denial (what do you mean, there's sand in the water?!), anger (if a clean person took a shower in this water, she'd come out needing a bath!), bargaining (how about if we give it three days and if the water hasn't cleared up, we move back to the UAE?), depression (I can't even take a decent shower; is that too much to ask?) and – finally – resignation (this is life now, Iman, so deal with it).

I headed to another grey room with a small bed. I was so exhausted I could've slept for the next decade, but I didn't. I spotted a spider's web stretched over the corner of my room. I had an unwanted room-mate. Despite having entomophobia, I didn't flinch, scream or run in circles like I usually do. *I bet you don't like it here either*, I thought (while squatting to get a closer look). I had never felt more pathetic, feeling a common bond with a spider because we both were helpless. But helpless creatures get crushed, and I vowed to not allow anything to crush me.

I woke up. One day down, eternity to go? The first thing I noticed was that I was sloshing in my own sweat. 'Who turned off the freaking fan?' I groused. I quickly discovered the power was out. (I would later learn that a shortage of fuel meant we had no electricity for up to eighteen hours a day.) As I inspected my environment, I was baffled by the strange kids staring at me.

'Shit,' I thought in alarm. 'Did I sleepwalk into someone else's house?'

'You look funny,' one of the kids said, pointing at my puffy eyes.

'Yeah, tell me about it,' I snapped. If I felt anything that morning – or, rather, afternoon, because I had slept for about sixteen hours – it was complete confusion.

I couldn't escape school. Still, I refused to spend money on a new uniform and borrowed my cousin's instead. On my first day, I donned the uniform, fighting back my tears. My parents took me to my new school in a taxi (very few people in Gaza can afford their own cars) and I hoped the tyres would blow so we could all go home. But, no, we arrived.

The school was small in comparison with the one I attended in the UAE. It was so old the blue paint had faded into grey. Considering my unfamiliarity with the surroundings, the principal thought it would be a good idea to assign me to my cousin's class. My cousin was a great help, I have to agree. At that point, she had to act as sort of a babysitter: she sat next to me in class, helped me with homework and even made sure I got home in a taxi.

'We're here,' she said, as we were dropped off close to my house. I headed east with a new-found sense of confidence, proud to have memorised the way home. But my cousin headed west and I'd nearly knocked on a complete stranger's door when she rectified the situation by yanking me by the elbow like I was a five-year-old.

Like any student who's endured a long day at school, I went straight to the kitchen. I was startled by what I found. Mum was lighting candles in the kitchen.

Me: 'Are we having a party? Conjuring spirits? Some special occasion I missed?'

Mum: 'No. The power is out, that's all.'

In Abu Dhabi, I had never imagined that people in the twenty-first century would use candles for any purpose other than topping a cake or having a romantic dinner. But I soon came to realise that people in Gaza weren't living in the same century as the rest of the world. The truth is, time in occupied war zones freezes. In Gaza, candles are needed to light a house – and they can also burn it down within minutes.

It was hard for my fifteen-year-old self to process the swift and drastic changes in my lifestyle. If I had to choose one sight in Gaza that was the most obviously different, it would be the streets. People of all ages rode donkeys, children sold peppermints and grown men stood all day at intersections trying to peddle cigarettes. Jobs and decent salaries are scarce, and this is the result. The streets also are where my dislike of Gaza developed into something greater – respect. People here are eager to learn and figure out how to thrive with very little. This proved to me that life was not over. It had just taken a different direction.

I stopped being fifteen the minute I set foot in Gaza. Doctor Strange would be stunned at my transition from a mere teenager to a not-so-naive young woman. At first, whenever I heard the call to prayer, I would grab my prayer rug and beseech God to take me back to the UAE. But in those early days, I was unable to hear God's answers. I knew deep down there must be a reason I had come to Gaza. I still don't know the reason, but I eventually trusted God, even as three successive Israeli assaults made me lose my faith in humans. I know for a fact that had He not placed me in this territory and tested me as I have been, I wouldn't have become the person I am today. I am thankful.

Iman chose not to provide an update on her status for this book.

A martyr for ever, caught on camera
by Haneen AbdAlnabi, mentored by Lea Gabay

It is estimated that as many as 250,000 Palestinians in Gaza participated in the Great Return March, a non-violent border protest that launched in the spring of 2018. Its goal was simple: to remind the world that the people of Gaza had been driven from their land by the Israelis, and that nothing else – including numerous UN resolutions and petitions to international courts – had worked to halt the blockade under which we now lived.

Many participants in the protest were from a new generation of Palestinian refugees, rediscovering the spirit of resistance that drove the First and Second Intifadas. One of them was Abed El-Fattah AbdAlnaby, aged eighteen. He was my second cousin.

Abed was among the first to be targeted by Israeli soldiers intent on stopping the protest – a number that since has grown to forty-nine. He was one of nine shot and killed by Israeli snipers the first day. And he achieved a kind of posthumous fame when what has now become an iconic photograph – taken moments before he was shot by Gazan photographer Mahmoud Abu Salama – appeared on the front page of *The Washington Post*. Here is the story behind that photo.

Abed El-Fattah was both the tallest and the youngest of the four sons in the family. (He also had five sisters!) He was known as a joker but was a quick learner in school with a special aptitude for maths. However, Abed left school when he was just sixteen to help support his family. He trained as a plumber and put in additional hours at a bakery, helping to pay one of his sisters' university tuition. He even bought his own clothes with his earnings.

Why did he decide to risk his life, meagre as it was, to not only participate in the protest but approach the front line? Abed's family members tell me he yearned to see his family's original village of Simsim, located just 15 kilometres (9.3 miles) northeast of Gaza. On 12 May 1948, pre-state Israeli forces ran the villagers out of their town. The concept of a daily march to the Gaza border to call for Palestinians' right to return to their ancestral homes captured his imagination, and he listened to news about the protest every day.

On 30 March, Abed awoke at 8 a.m. and worked at his brother's falafel restaurant until around two in the afternoon. Then he went home for his lunch but didn't eat much. Instead, he prepared himself for the march, putting on new clothes he had purchased the day before. It was as if he wanted to look like a gentleman for what would become the day of his death. Once dressed, he left home in a taxi. His friends next door (Zyed Abu Oukar and Yousef Masoud) and his brother Muhammad, with whom he was very close, followed shortly after.

Many of the protesters carried tyres, which had become a symbol of the First and Second Intifadas. Tyres were used at that time to block the vans driven by Zionist soldiers. But this time, many among the thousands gathered along the border burned the tyres to obscure the view of the Israeli snipers, who targeted them with live ammunition.

According to Muhammad, Abed El-Fattah did not initially join the protesters at the front. However, when snipers began shooting at a younger boy carrying a tyre close to the border fence, he darted forward and grabbed it from him so the teen could run faster. Both were running back towards the crowd of demonstrators when Israeli snipers shot five bullets. One hit Muhammad, who was close by; he was spared only because the bullet was deflected by the mobile phone in his front shirt pocket. Another hit Abed in the head. He was rushed to a hospital, but he could not be saved.

'My soul was taken from me,' his father says.

How do you begin to describe such a loss? I could write about his grieving family and friends, who are haunted by his memory. Or I could describe the community mosque and his sister's house, both of which he helped build. Or I could interview Fadwa, an elderly woman in the neighbourhood who can't walk, so she uses a wheelchair. Abed knew she had no children to look after her, so became her surrogate son, bringing her food and helping her with chores almost every day. Now, she moans about how deeply she misses him.

'He is still with us, though, because he is in our hearts,' says his mother with tears in her eyes.

And despite their bottomless grief, his brothers continue to participate in the march with their father, in the hope that change will come, and that maybe, just maybe, they can see Simsim.

Haneen, her youngest sister and her mother managed to make it to the United States and then to Canada before Israel launched its genocide. They hope to earn permanent residence and then bring the rest of the family to join them.

A journalist grows up
by Manar Alsheikh, mentored by Deborah Root

A teenage girl carried a camera as she approached the field by the border to photograph protesters in Gaza's Great Return March. She gathered her hair with a red tie and began to run, surrounded by the smoke of burning tyres, heading towards the two young men about to scale the fence. She was intent only on capturing the scene in a photo. It was like something out of a Hollywood movie, with the heroine conquering her fear to follow her dreams and serve her people.

The heroine of this story is Menna Murad Qudiah, fourteen, a girl with deep brown eyes and smooth, rosy skin. She lives in Khuza'a – the site of one of the worst attacks of the 2014 Israeli war against Gaza – and is the youngest journalist to report on the historic, non-violent protest calling for the right of Palestinians to return to their ancestral homeland.

Menna's main love is photography, thanks to her Uncle Ihab, a journalist who allowed her to experiment with his camera when she was just four years old. But she has many talents: fashion design, poetry reciting, acting and playing piano. Menna is a born performer. She played in a piano recital at the A.M. Qattan Foundation in Gaza City, and her Uncle Ihab filmed her as she sang and recited patriotic poems on the roof of her home during the 2014 Israeli assault. Her deep yet soft voice was interrupted by the sound of missiles and raids, but she never stopped singing.

Menna was eager to participate as soon as word of the Great Return March spread, and she smiled broadly as she recalled how she couldn't sleep the night before the first day of the protest, almost as if she was about to go on a school trip. She wasn't afraid, she says; she was excited. She was a regular participant after that, attending with members of her family: her father, brothers, sometimes her grandfather – and, of course, Uncle Ihab.

An editor for a Saudi Arabian newspaper and a member of the International Federation of Journalists, Ihab had long acted as a mentor to Menna. Because he believes in her flair for photography, he lends her his own camera. Her father also is a faithful supporter. Even though he does not receive his salary for months at a time, he pays for her to take workshops in journalism.

Detecting that I was wondering about the effect of the protests on her studies, Menna raised her right eyebrow and shook her index finger, admonishing: 'Don't worry; I won first place in a contest sponsored by the Ministry of Education for beginning broadcasters.' And then there was a challenge by her history teacher. He asked her to answer three difficult questions, and she answered them all. She turned her room upside down searching for her school schedule to show me. And like any normal early teen, she had decorated it with Hello Kitty stickers.

One day at the protest, Menna inhaled tear gas, causing her eyes, nose and throat to sting and swell. A volunteer paramedic, 21-year-old Razan Alnajjar, rushed to her aid. Later, Menna learned that Razan had been shot by an Israeli sniper while coming to the aid of a protester.

And then there was Yasser Murtaja. It was the morning of 4 April when Menna met Yasser, a well-known and loved journalist covering the protests. He kindly let her look into the lens of his sophisticated camera and showed her how to use it. When Menna showed him her own photos of the protesters, he raised his eyebrows in appreciation, and said her work was equal to that of professional photographers. Then he suggested making a film about her youthful skill and bravery. When she heard his words, her heart soared.

On the day they were scheduled to shoot the short film, Menna told Yasser she needed to finish early because she had homework to do. He smiled and said: 'Your camera and your books will scare the soldiers more than any weapons, so do your homework.' Instead, he filmed her as she completed her assignments. Sadly, however, the documentary had to be completed by other crew members from the Ain Media production company, where Yasser worked. Yasser was shot by an Israeli sniper while covering the second Friday of the Great Return March – a wound that resulted in his death on

6 April. He left behind his son, many friends – and his camera. Her mother told me Menna couldn't cry in front of her father and brothers; instead, when she heard the news, she escaped to her room to sob.

Her emotions were still raw when her teacher criticised Yasser in class because she thought he had not worn a protective vest. Menna raised her hand to speak and corrected the teacher, insisting that he had indeed worn his flak jacket. Her teacher challenged her, asking: 'How do you know?' Menna replied that she went to the protest daily and was in fact the youngest journalist covering the Great Return March. The entire class, including the teacher, laughed at her in disbelief. Menna left the class in tears.

This incident at first made Menna feel like giving up. But she knew if she didn't believe in herself, no one else would. She remembered Yasser playing the funny clown, snatching her camera and then fleeing. She remembered the ululating call of the men when they dragged down the barbed-wire fence that penned her people in. She recalled her interview with an old, Bedouin woman, who had been born in Bir al-Saba and forcibly displaced by Israeli gangs in 1948, forcing her to live in Gaza's camps. She had promised this old woman to keep smiling, because a smile is a gesture of defiance, telling Israeli snipers they won't defeat the Palestinians of Gaza.

Menna believes in the saying: 'Success is a simple measurement of the commitment, sacrifice and pain one endures to achieve a dream.' So, she continues to work towards her dream of becoming a professional journalist. She now works for an online radio station in Khan Younis, saving money to buy her own camera.

And when Menna met the old Bedouin woman once again, the first thing she did was to hug her and say: 'Thank you for saving me.'

Manar remains in northern Gaza, an area Israel is intent on 'cleansing', with her mother and three of her brothers. A fourth brother was killed in May 2024. 'We are afraid to try to leave the north because my mother is sick and has difficulty walking, and because the Israelis arrest so many of the young men they find,' she says. 'I don't want to lose my other brothers.'

My day of reckoning at the Great Return March
by Zahra Shaikhah, mentored by Mary Simkins

On what has become known as Burning-Tyre Friday, I had planned to run on the beach to reduce my stress. I never thought fate had something else in mind for me that day – to tempt, and run from, Israeli bullets during Gaza's Great Return March.

I always study for my English literature classes on Friday mornings, but that day I couldn't. How could I study French philosopher Jacques Derrida when my brain was spinning and couldn't concentrate?

A group of We Are Not Numbers writers invited me to go along with them to the protest to shoot a video about the march. I didn't hesitate to say yes. Yet, a feeling of 'bad things could happen' nagged at me. The protest had kicked off the week before, and sixteen of our young men had been shot and killed by Israeli snipers in one day! More than 1,400 others were wounded or fainted from tear gas. I must be honest, if my fellow team members hadn't encouraged me, I wouldn't have gone! Would I come back as a dead body or, worse, a disabled 21-year-old girl?

My dad is different from many other fathers in Gaza, who keep their daughters at home to protect them. He raised me to be independent, saying I must be the one who 'saves' myself. He never tells me 'no' when I ask him if I can go somewhere or do something; he gives me advice and we discuss it when he thinks I am wrong or has concerns, but he trusts and respects me. So, he allowed me to go when I said I wanted to visit the march.

We went to one of the five protest encampments: Shujaiya, on the eastern border of Gaza; its translation is literally 'bravery'. It was almost noon and the people of Gaza were getting ready for the *Jummah* prayer, which is performed every Friday. I texted my brother's wife, who lives in our same building, to bring my seven-month-old niece Hanan, which means 'kindness'. Thinking I might not come back, I wanted to say goodbye to the person I love the most.

I hugged Hanan and kissed her right cheek, whispering: 'I love you.' She was so soft and calm, and her warmth in my arms softened my heart so I could mentally forgive everyone who had hurt me in case I never came back or returned no longer whole. Earlier in the morning, my sister Amal (which means hope) called to warn me: our late mother visited in her dream, telling her not to lose her younger sister.

'You have dreams to achieve. You are an excellent student who is about to graduate and complete your master's in literature. I cannot afford to lose you! Firas [her son] and I need you! Those Israelis don't care if you are near the fence or not; they just shoot!'

Amal beseeched me. But my desire to be with my

friends and show solidarity with my people were strong, and I donned comfortable shoes so I could run at any moment. To calm my nerves, I played a Palestinian song that taunts Israeli soldiers, warning of the traps we will set for them if they enter Gaza. Standing in front of the mirror, I put on my headscarf, looked myself in the eye and said: *I have nothing to lose* (even though I did). I took my bag, into which I had stuffed my literature book that discussed Jacques Derrida, and left.

At the march, we walked among the crowd holding the signs we had made for the video we planned to shoot for We Are Not Numbers, expressing solidarity with the protest. As we moved forward, we were ever closer to the tyres set on fire to obscure the vision of the Israeli snipers. Trolleys from which ice cream, chips and sandwiches were sold were at the back of the march, next to the tents with families. It was like a festival! People laughed, talked and took photos. The fear was on the other side, among the Israeli soldiers, not ours.

We looked for a good spot to start filming. As we settled in a place among the protesters, I watched with fascination the brave boys, men and a few women at the front lines. Then suddenly, those men were running away from the Israeli 'security fence'. I didn't realise at first that death itself was chasing them, in the form of bullets and tear gas grenades. Dreamlike, I heard a voice telling me and Haneen, my best friend: 'Run, girls.' Convinced it was the angel of death about to visit us too, I ran. My subconscious blocked the memory of what happened next. I remember nothing clearly, not even how I felt. All I recall very well was reaching a safe place, where I lost my balance and tripped. When I got up, my lungs felt like they were about to explode.

I was about to scream or laugh, I'm not sure which, when my eyes settled on Haneen. She was sobbing, with a frozen, horrified look. I rushed to hold her.

'We are fine, Haneen. We are fine,' I consoled her. 'We are not dead; we haven't died.'

Two men came to check on us. One was bald, wearing a blue shirt and I would guess was almost forty years old; the other was tall with black hair in his late thirties. 'You were the best girls who ran,' said the first one, joking. The other man brought a bottle of water for Haneen to drink. After her panic attack eased and Haneen regained her sense of balance, I broke into hysterical laughter.

Together with my friends, I witnessed the sunset while other protesters, undaunted, returned to the fence, not caring about the snipers. Once at home, I wasn't sure how I felt. Was it a good or bad decision to go to the march? The moment I put my head on my pillow and closed my eyes, I remembered seeing the yellow-green land moving fast beneath my running feet. My head felt heavy and thick recalling the trauma, and I fell asleep.

Ever since that day, I have felt an energy running in my blood and a blossoming of life warming my heart.

Every morning, I remind myself that I lived! There is hope! No hardship can break me down. Not any more.

Zahra is studying for her master's degree in international relations in Turkey, but her family remain in Gaza. Her house has been partially destroyed and her uncle and two cousins have been killed.

Ramadan in Gaza is different this year
by Orjwan Shurrab, mentored by Mimi Kirk

I was almost eleven when I first accompanied my mother to al-Zawiya market, one of the oldest and biggest and located in the centre of Gaza City, to buy food for Ramadan. I remember how fascinated I was by the old buildings, the mountains of fruit and vegetables with their bright colours, the aroma of spices, the Sun's rays filtering in. My mother laughed as my eyes roved around and I touched everything I could reach. She told every seller it was my first time there.

My mother loves my name, and likes to call for me in a loud, clear voice so that others will ask her about it. Orjwan is not a common name in Gaza; in fact, I've never met anyone here who shares it with me. It is the word for the dye the Phoenicians extracted from Mediterranean oysters to colour their clothes – a mix of red, orange and purple. That day, my mother called my name repeatedly and I do believe if I were to go to the market again and the old man selling herbs in one of the corners was still there, he would remember me once I say my name.

Our first visit to the market was in 2007, the year after Hamas took over the Strip. People here were relatively better off then than they are now, since some residents still had independent sources of income. The Israeli blockade, imposed to punish Hamas but penalising all 2 million residents, was in its first year and the private sector was still strong.

But now, after eleven years of the blockade, life for Gazans has become untenable. Even the employees of the Palestinian Authority (PA), who for so long were guaranteed salaries, are no longer getting paid their full pay. (My mother, who is my family's sole earner, is a PA employee and didn't receive anything in April. This month, she got half of her pay, and we have no idea what to expect in June.) About half of all adults are unemployed, and even more youths are without jobs. No one has the capacity to cope with any new hardship.

As a result, Ramadan feels totally different this year from the happy memories of my childhood. With the electricity crisis so extreme, my mother cannot buy the special holiday meats and cheeses a month in advance like she used to do, since our refrigerator cannot keep anything fresh. Three hours a day of refrigeration is not enough, particularly on steaming summer days. Instead, we must shop daily and the market is far away. The trip to the market also is expensive, even for just a weekly trip. (Unlike in countries in the West, most Gazans don't have cars. It would require 12 shekels, or £2.50, for my mom and I to take a taxi each time, plus whatever we tip the driver to help us load the bags. While that may not seem a lot of money to you, it is to us here.) Instead, we buy what we need daily from nearby shops.

A local newspaper recently published photos of al-Zawiya with the headline: 'Gaza Markets Prepare for the Arrival of Ramadan.' Outsiders would not be able to tell how things are different today, but I can. Although the sellers have stocked their shops as always, with the fruit and vegetables arranged the same way as when I was eleven, what I saw in the images broke my heart. I saw a very small number of people in the market, with the vendors having plenty of time to sit for photos. I remembered how crowded the market used to be and how many times we had to repeat what we needed so the sellers could hear us above the clamour!

As if this is not enough pain, 120 families are without their loved ones this Ramadan, and more than 13,000 others are at the bedsides of relatives who were injured by Israeli snipers during the ongoing Great Return March. While every Ramadan Palestinian families in Gaza mourn loved ones who have been killed in past Israeli attacks, this year the number of grieving families is increasing during the holiday itself.

After *iftar*, the meal at which Muslims break their fast, children typically go into the streets to play. Just a few minutes after the *adhan*, or call to prayer, announces it is time to break the fast, they finish their meals and head out, their voices echoing against the cement walls until midnight. This year, however, I do not hear them.

They seem to be too busy mourning the losses in their families.

The enthusiasm with which I usually welcome this month each year is gone. The anticipation of what my mother will cook for *iftar* is gone. In its place is a feeling of nothingness and depression. I feel pain each time I watch the news and learn someone new has died of his wounds, or another has been injured.

These tragedies, in tandem with the rising poverty and unemployment rates that distinguish this tiny strip of land, have killed the taste for life in Gaza.

Orjwan managed to escape from Gaza to Egypt, where she now lives with her husband and two children. Her youngest child was born in Cairo, and thus does not have a proper Palestinian birth certificate. She is told that must wait until the end of the endless war. Meanwhile, she agonises over her family left behind.

The cost of protest
by Mahmoud Alnaouq, mentored by Louisa Waugh

In the early mornings on my way to college, I used to see Yaser Alaklouk on his way to his job, wearing his work clothes and carrying a spade or shovel in his hand. We walked together to the end of the road, talking about my university studies and his job, my parents and his kids. At the end of the street, both of us went our own ways, wishing each other good luck, as we do in Gaza.

Yaser's difficult life was reflected in the way he looked. Since his graduation from high school, he laboured as a farmhand or construction worker – wherever and whenever he could get a job. At the age of thirty-four, he looked more like fifty-five; white hairs sprouted amid his black strands, wrinkles etched deep grooves in his face.

About five months ago, one of our neighbours stopped me and said: 'Yaser is in the hospital in very bad condition.' I was so shocked I was speechless. Yaser, I learned, had been shot while participating in the Great Return March. His left leg had been shattered by one of those exploding bullets we'd been hearing about that struck fear into our hearts.

The news spread rapidly across our neighbourhood in Deir al-Balah, located in the middle of the Gaza Strip.

Everyone prayed for him. His relatives, neighbours and friends crowded into the hospital, all wanting to show their support for him and his family.

Yaser lay in the hospital for three weeks until he was released. I thought the worst was over, but I was wrong. His neighbours told me they awakened every night to the sound of him screaming in pain. I knew I had to visit him. He was so glad to see me, and to share his story.

Yaser, his wife and four kids (ages five to fifteen) had participated in the protest east of the al-Bureij refugee camp every Friday since it began on 30 March. Al-Bureij, which is also in the middle area of Gaza, is one of the five areas that 'hosts' the Great Return March. Every time I went to the march, I'd see Yaser either on the bus that transports people to the protest or at the event itself.

He told me that all he really wanted in life is to provide a decent living for his family and watch his kids grow up safely. He hoped that if the Great Return March persisted, Israel might be forced to ease up on its blockade of Gaza.

Yaser and his eldest son used to sit on a small hill near the front line of the protest, watching young men hurl rocks at the soldiers and children wave flags. His wife and his other three kids didn't want to risk being shot, so they stayed in the women's tent, behind a tall sand hill.

27 April, the fifth Friday of the march, was no different from any other 'protest Friday'.

Protesters who had been shot on previous days

showed up in splints and on crutches. Haggling vendors were there too; they never missed a single Friday, happy with the prospect of earning extra money by selling ice cream, cans of soda and nuts. Music blasted from speakers, playing patriotic songs. They never got old, although the people had heard the lyrics a million times.

That Friday ended differently, however. Yaser was sitting on a sand dune, dreaming of returning to his family's historic homeland.

Then, an explosion ripped the air, sounding very close. At first, Yaser thought it was the sound of a tear gas bomb. 'I tried to stand up, but I couldn't. I looked down at my legs and saw that the left one was a mass of blood and torn flesh,' Yaser told me, recalling the shock.

He had been shot by a type of bullet that explodes inside the body. His leg bones were shattered and most of the flesh was pulverised.

The other protesters around Yaser carried him to a nearby ambulance on standby. He arrived at a local hospital in Deir al-Balah, but was quickly transferred to the intensive care unit at Shifa Hospital in Gaza City, the largest medical complex in Gaza.

Yaser needed thirty-six units of blood, or about 14.5 litres. He has had two surgeries and has another to go. Fortunately, he escaped amputation, but will never be able to walk normally again.

Yaser struggled to hide his pain and depression, but his eyes told me everything as he admitted he now depends on humanitarian aid to live. He can no longer work. And that is not what Yaser, or any other man, wants for himself and his family.

'Do you regret going to the march?' I asked. 'No! Never.' He answered in a clear, strong voice. 'Why would I regret it? I didn't do anything wrong. And I still go to the march every Friday.'

In 2023, Mahmoud, Ahmed Alnaouq's brother, achieved his dream: he won a scholarship to pursue a master's degree at the University of Melbourne. However, before he could travel to Australia, he was killed. At 4.30 a.m. on 22 October 2023, the home where he was sleeping with twenty other members of his family was bombed by Israeli forces. They died instantly. In May 2024, student protesters at the University of Melbourne renamed the Arts West building Mahmoud's Hall.

Gazans send kites over the border
by Ahmed Alnaouq, mentored by Pam Bailey

While the Israeli media decry the use of kites to send Molotov cocktails over the border from the Gaza Strip, the most common use of kites by Palestinians is a peaceful one. Kites have flown throughout Gaza's Great Return March protest along the Israeli border. As the Palestinian author Ramzy Baroud, who grew up in one of Gaza's refugee camps, once wrote: 'People living under oppressive rules take every opportunity to express defiance, even through [only] symbolic ways.' Kites have long been one of those symbols because, unlike the Palestinians in Gaza, they can fly free – high above the blockaded borders.

One group of Palestinian youths and young adults set out to make and fly 1,000 kites in the colours of their national flag (red, green and white). 'I wanted to show the world we are peacefully protesting and rejecting any idea of violence,' explained 29-year-old Rami Siam, a father of three who sells children's toys from a stand in Gaza City. The idea for the kite project was his, inspired when he heard some Israelis describe the Great Return March on TV as violent and manipulated by Hamas.

Siam recruited fifteen other volunteers, aged twelve

to sixty, who met in the courtyard of the 800-year-old al-Ajami Mosque in the heart of old Gaza City to make kites and do their part to send a message of 'peace and hope'. 'We chose the mosque because we grew up in this neighbourhood and our families spent so much time here,' Siam said. 'It brings back memories of our childhoods and reminds us of our ancestors, who prayed here as well.' It also was the only place possible to meet all day for a week, free. A core group worked at their task starting right after the dawn prayer (6 a.m.) until it became dark – breaking only for lunch. Others, who sold goods from street carts, came after work or during breaks. Still others came after school.

The participants grouped themselves into different corners of the mosque's courtyard, with each responsible for a part of the process: cutting the sticks, measuring the spaces between them and tying them into the shape of the kite's skeleton; glueing on the coloured paper that formed the body; affixing the tail; and shaping and attaching the *sharasheeb* (wings above the tail). On some of the kites, they painted the flags of Arab countries to solicit their support. On others, a calligraphy artist wrote the names of erased Palestinian towns or Gazans who have been killed by Israeli snipers during the protest. The plan: to cut their 'tethers' once they were in the sky, so the kites could sail over the separation fence and into the land of the victims' heritage. They weren't able to see Palestine when they were alive, but the kites would carry them there, in spirit.

'Since we can't reach our stolen lands, we are going to fly our kites over them,' affirmed nineteen-year-old Moab Fazaa. 'We write these names to remind the world and ourselves that we will never forget our martyrs or our villages.'

This dream unites all Palestinians, bringing them together across all religious factions and beliefs. That, and the tradition of kite-making. 'I remember I used to make kites when I was young; I was taught this by my father and grandfather,' said Abu Mohammed, who is nearly sixty years old. Siam added that while it might seem easy to make a kite, it requires a lot of concentration because any mistake makes it unflyable.

'When we started to implement this project, I was surprised at the level of support we attracted, with everyone in the neighbourhood praising our work and even helping us with what they could,' Siam added. On some days, the number of participants reached forty.

'We only left when we were too exhausted to do more; we love this work and we think we are sending an important message,' said Abu Alabed, forty, one of the organisers.

In the end, the team made about 300 kites, and on the first day they were brought to the march, the children were so excited by the sight, they trampled most of them. However, Siam and his recruits saved some and made new ones – and this time they flew. Their kites sailed right over the border to Palestine, and freedom.

CHAPTER FIVE
2019

The world is my room
by Basman Derawi, mentored by Pam Bailey

The world is my room;
it is the place I know the best,
the only place where I can
speak up and scream,
the only place I feel
somehow safe.

A drone is living
over my head
and I can't get
the sound of oppression
out of my ears.
I close my eyes
and deeply breathe,
trying to purge the fear
from my mind,
the prickles from my skin.

I draw a peaceful sky
on my ceiling,
with tranquil planets,
Sun and Moon:

A night with no scary thoughts –
Their 'sticks and stones'
is the language of oppression.

Basman was in Egypt, pursuing advanced training as a physiotherapist, when the Israeli genocide began. The rest of his family managed to join him except for his sister, Eman, who was killed along with her husband and four children. Basman and his family now await the end of the destruction so they can return home. In addition to Eman and her family, Basman has lost two close friends – Essa and Ouda – to the war. And it is to them that he dedicates all of his poems going forward.

Reaching for the stars
by Abdallah Abusamra, mentored by Pam Bailey

When I was a kid, I often asked my parents about the lights that seemed to 'wander' in the night sky. 'Who switches them on?' I asked my father. He'd look at me blankly, as if he had not heard me; if I asked again, he would light a cigarette and preoccupy himself with the smoke circles. My mother then would say: 'Come on, Abood! I have told you a thousand times! GOD SWITCHES THEM ON AT NIGHT.' I did not understand how God did that, so her answer never quite satisfied me. Nonetheless, I enjoyed telling others that 'GOD SWITCHES THE STARS ON AT NIGHT'.

My friend, Bahaa Elhabeel, however, decided to figure out the answer himself by making telescopes and studying pictures of the Moon, stars and constellations. He developed a deep passion for science, which is remarkable in Gaza, since science is not a priority unless you're studying medicine. (While science is taught in schools, only the most basic of lab equipment is available. More 'creative' subjects like astronomy are neglected altogether.)

Bahaa recalls: 'The first time I gazed at those little things illuminating the sky, I felt literally close to them. I remember asking my parents: "What are they? Why don't they fall down?"

'But their answers were pure nonsense to me. They would say merely that those are the stars, and they can't fall because they dwell there. Every answer I got from my parents prompted me to ask more sophisticated questions, until they could not answer any more. I then figured something out: if the stars can't come down to me, maybe I could go up to them. Since that time, I have engaged in my quest. I wanted to know the components of the stars and planets, if they move and the orbits they follow, the forces that stop them from falling and everything else about them.'

After conducting research for many months on the internet and through dozens of books, Bahaa was most inspired by a volume titled *Optix*, which included diagrams for making telescopes. At the age of thirteen, he made his first telescope, using materials such as water pipes and scrap metal. His simple telescope enabled him to see the Moon closer up. However, he still wasn't satisfied. Bahaa couldn't see the stars, Moon and other planets with the kind of resolution that would mimic holding them in his hands. He made another telescope, with clearer resolution, one year later.

'This one was a reflecting telescope [which uses one or more curved mirrors with larger diameters than other kinds], like Galileo's,' Bahaa explained. 'I could see the Moon far better. Now, I wanted to collaborate with others, which is the true spirit of science. But since I am a Palestinian living in Gaza, we are not allowed to travel or even receive visitors.'

Instead, Bahaa offered to share his telescopes with local educational institutions, for use by students interested in observing the night sky.

'I hoped my scopes would attract students to come and see the Moon and stars, but I was not taken seriously. I was not invited to schools or science fairs in Gaza. People did not share my passion. I started to isolate myself. I allowed my grades at school to suffer and began to hate myself.'

Despite the stigma that prevents many Palestinians from seeking mental health help, Bahaa finally visited a psychiatrist. He was diagnosed with severe depression.

'I thought death would be better than not being able to pursue a meaningful future. If I continued working on my own, I would lack the research labs, facilities, materials and equipment essential to my work; it's almost impossible to obtain specialised equipment because of the Israeli blockade,' he explained.

However, with the help of his psychiatrist, Bahaa recovered his passion and got back on track. That's when a professor and manager of the al-Aqsa TV channel's research centre noticed Bahaa's work and offered him an unpaid internship.

'[Through that opportunity,] I learned so much. I bought books and became absorbed with reading. I discovered stars and planets I didn't know about before,' Bahaa said.

While working at the research centre, Bahaa heard about

a contest for scientific inventions; the winner would be awarded a fully funded scholarship to study in the United States. For his entry, Bahaa built a specialised telescope that could detect radio emissions from natural, celestial objects or artificial satellites. It won. However, he says, the design – and thus, the credit – was assigned to someone else with better connections. Bahaa sank into another depression; his mother recalled that he stopped eating and talking, sleeping most of the time instead. And again, he bounced back... although it took longer this time.

Still at the al-Aqsa centre, Bahaa built an eight-inch telescope through which he could see the stars of the Pleiades (Seven Sisters) and Messier 30 clusters. He also wrote a book about the need to save the Earth from overproduction of carbon dioxide and create solar-power collection systems as sources of renewable energy – all while he was still in high school.

Today, Bahaa is in his *tawjihi* year of school – the final year before university that determines so much of a young Palestinian's future. For now, he has had to put astronomy aside as he studies.

'I have to stop doing the stuff I'm in love with, so I can earn a high grade average in a major I'm not really interested in. Dynamic astronomy is not a field of study available in Gaza,' he said sadly.

Bahaa is not giving up on his passion, however. Despite the limitations imposed by the Israeli blockade, the lack of resources in Gaza and the cultural barriers, he continues his research. Someday, he knows, he will make it to the United States and study his chosen field with the experts. It's just a matter of time, perseverance – and a little bit of luck. His time will come.

The time finally came for both Abdallah and Bahaa to achieve their dreams. Abdallah is studying in Ireland, and although he is not in the United States, Bahaa is pursuing astronomy in Russia.

The gift of shared suffering
by Neda Abadla, mentored by Adiel Suarez-Murias

Every day, I meet people living their most vulnerable and painful moments. I feel their suffering, and each day I gather all my strength to hear and feel their pain. It is my job. I joined the administrative team for MSF (Médecins Sans Frontières, or Doctors Without Borders) in July 2018.

Since March of last year, MSF has intensified its work in the Gaza Strip in response to the swelling number of people injured by sniper fire and tear gas in the Great Return March. Today, most of MSF's work is emergency care, as well as physical and occupational therapy for burn patients. My job is to receive patients and their families when they first enter the clinic. And it's simultaneously the most satisfying and painful experience I have ever had. I share the desperation, fear and hopelessness so obvious in the eyes of parents as they face the mortality of their injured children. I feel the pain of people with burns that have caused their skin and tissue to literally melt to the bone. I imagine the phantom pain felt by young men whose legs must be amputated and are shocked when they still experience agony in the empty space where their limbs used to be. Every day, when I go home to my family, a lingering shadow of that pain stays with me.

I will never forget the day I saw a man in the clinic crying and cradling his two-year-old son, his whole body shaking. When the electricity shuts off, as it does for an average of eight hours a day right now, many families make small fires to cook or for heat. His son, Adam, was deeply burned in his groin area. The little boy had already developed septicaemia, an infection that spreads rapidly throughout the body. He was referred immediately to the department MSF operates in Gaza City's Shifa Hospital.

We called Adam's father every day to check on him, but it was hard to hear the man's voice through his tears. Several days after we transferred him, Adam slipped into a coma. When we called his father with the news, he begged: 'Please pray for him.' When Adam died, I too was in shock. 'How can he die?' I asked myself, knowing there was no answer. What I remember most about that day is the father's voice when he told us: 'You did what you can do, and I am so thankful for that.' I was speechless. I wished then that I had supernatural powers and could change reality.

A part of me died with Adam that day. I think it is the part that used to believe that children are immortal; that they don't suffer or die!

But, even as a part of my heart died that day, I found reason to hope through Milaina Alhendi, a protester in the Great Return March who had been shot in her leg by an Israeli soldier on the western border of Khan Younis. Milaina is a wife and mother of six. She told me her son and her husband had been shot in the protest as well. When she returned to the clinic, she responded to my obvious concern about her limping gait with a smile in her eyes that inspired me to smile back.

Despite Milaina's complex injury, she continued with her daily chores for her family. And still she protested at the border, demanding her right to return to her ancestral homeland. I once asked: 'How can you keep going on with your daily routine? How can you live or even sleep with pins in your leg?' (Her treatment included what is called 'external fixation', performed to immobilise fractured bones and allow them to heal properly. Pins or screws are driven into the bone on both sides of the fracture, then secured together using external clamps and rods.) It was obvious to me that she was in pain, yet Milaina said: 'This is nothing. I can deal with it easily.'

Milaina is a strong, determined woman, and in those qualities I see beauty. While some die of pain, others discover their own strength.

Even though my work is exhausting, there is much to love. The best part of my workday is soothing burned children, distracting them from their pain by blowing up balloons. Working with MSF has also given me an opportunity unique among most Palestinians from Gaza: to meet internationals from around the world during their missions here. They add to my character, and I add to theirs. Last year, at Christmas, we organised a small goodbye party for Jennifer, the nursing manager for the MSF office here. It was only a couple of hours, but during that space of time, all borders, nationalities, religions and customs that stand between people melted away; we forgot who we are and where we 'belong'. I forgot that I am imprisoned in Gaza, and that is quite a gift.

Neda, her husband and her two children now live in Turkey, where they work at various jobs.

My battlefield is my brain
by Iman Inshasi, mentored by Deborah Root

When I tell people I have a migraine, they shrug and say: 'Why don't you just take a painkiller?' As if painkillers are magic beans that instantly heal – and as if I haven't taken loads of them already.

When a migraine moves into my brain and takes up residence, I'm paralysed. I can't move, eat or do anything that produces any sort of sound. Anyone who enters my room during a migraine episode would likely mistake it for a vampire's nest. Light blinds me, so my curtains are drawn, the lamps are turned off and not a single sound is allowed. A mandatory hush cloaks our entire house.

I wallow in my bed, waiting for the drugs to kick in. It takes a while – if they work at all. It feels like two little genies are playing jump-rope with the nerve above my right eye. The genies refuse to stop, taunting me even when I cry. It's their playtime and my crying time. If I try to open my eyes and scan the room, my vision is blurry. I close my eyes. Life becomes dark when I'm in pain, literally.

I remember the time I had a migraine for over six hours. I wished I were some kind of inanimate object, like a table. Tables are static and don't possess human feelings. The pain throbbed so much I let go of all my dreams for the future. I found them inane and trivial. My only wish was for the migraine to go away.

When I was a child, I watched my mother endure the same ordeal. At first, I knew only that she was sick, and to me that meant she had a fever. So, I would open the fridge, grab a bottle of cold water and pour it on a towel. I placed the wet towel on her forehead while squatting next to her and waited for the fever to go away. Little did I know then, it wasn't fever. Rather, Mum's brain was on fire.

Later, when I learned the truth of her affliction, I decided to become a neurologist. But I hate maths. Sorry, Mum. And I followed in her footsteps, at the unusually early age of thirteen or fourteen.

Gaza is hell for everyone who lives here, but especially for people who have migraines. When desperately trying to fall asleep at 5 a.m., it is particularly nightmarish to hear hawkers screaming at the top of their lungs: 'Broken fridges for sale!' Covering your ears doesn't help when the neighbouring kids decide to stage their own World Cup match right outside your window at 7 a.m.

My mouth has a bad taste too when my migraines strike, sort of like a bitter aftertaste that lingers for ever. I think how hungry I am, but simultaneously, the very thought of food turns my stomach. Plus, the act of chewing is torturous. Anything crunching or sliding between my upper and lower teeth sounds to me like stones grinding against bone. So I starve.

My whole day is on pause, waiting for the throbbing

to go away. I shrink into my bed, as if making my body small is going to stop the pain from spreading. Houses are too close here and sometimes I can hear the next-door family's entire conversation. When I have a migraine, I can even hear fingernails being trimmed.

Due to the Israeli blockade, it's impossible to find the specialised migraine painkillers I read about. And even if they were available, a single pill would cost over £10. Most of us can't afford it.

My last resort becomes the ER. After I get there, I wait, wait and wait some more. I feel as if I am in a beehive. I hear moans of pain. It's so damn bright. A vampire shouldn't be there. The place smells like vomit. White lab coats move around constantly. At last, a nurse who's been on his feet for eight hours asks me in an impatient, condescending tone: 'What's wrong with our patient?'

I plead: 'Can you please dim the lights a little?'

A stronger combination of painkillers is infused into my left arm. I'm not bleeding in the wake of a bombing; I've not been mutilated by Israeli sniper fire at the Great Return March. 'You shouldn't be in the ER,' I know everyone is thinking.

Tell that to my fried brain.

A senseless death in Turkey
by Issam Adwan, mentored by Pam Bailey

It's common knowledge that a large number of Gazan youths dream of emigrating. Except we think of it as 'escaping' – as if from prison. What is not as well known is what happens afterwards – if and when Palestinians manage to make it to what they imagine will be a better place. Too often, Palestinians are treated like pariahs everywhere they go. My friend Mohammed Shamla learned this first-hand:

Mohammed, twenty-five, lived in Nuseirat Camp in the middle part of the Gaza Strip. The oldest son, he had three sisters and four younger brothers. I met him at Gaza City's al-Aqsa University, where we both studied English. Our first time getting to know each other was at a football match during the play-off competition among the university's various departments. I discovered he was in love with the sport as much as I was and was even better as a midfield player. He was selected to play that position and I was his back-up. My other overriding memory of him is his smile. He seemed to smile all the time, no matter how harsh things got in Gaza.

After his graduation, we didn't get together in person much, since I live in Rafah to the far south, but we chatted regularly on Facebook. He was unable to get a decent job and was ashamed of having to take pocket money from his father. Like so many other youths, he became obsessed with travelling abroad to find a better life.

Turkey is one of the few countries willing to give Palestinians a visa without a proven scholarship or job, and Mohammed secured that without much problem. But because of the blockade imposed on Gaza by both Israel and Egypt, he could only leave the Strip by paying a bribe, a fortune for most Gazans, to win a place on the exit list for the Rafah crossing. Even after paying, he was denied permission to exit a few times due to the bad relations between Egypt and Turkey. Finally, he was allowed to leave.

Mohammed's ultimate plan was to find a smuggler to help him get to Greece. Until then, he and other migrants lived in a cheap hotel. He stayed there for ten weeks, until 3 April. On that day, Mohammed fell from the fourth floor of his Izmir hotel, cracking his skull and putting him into a coma. Today, 12 April, he succumbed to his wounds and died in an intensive care unit. If our only source of information was Turkish officials, it would be known as a tragic accident after the police were forced to chase him for 'illegal activities'. The truth, however, is dramatically different.

One of his friends who lived in the hotel with him, but is too scared to talk publicly, says Mohammed and other refugees and migrants often were chased by the Turkish police despite carrying documents allowing them to be in the country. The purpose was to exploit them by making them pay a bribe. On 4 April, the police raided some of the hotel rooms using tear gas, forcing Mohammed to attempt to escape to another room via the balcony. He slipped and fell to the ground – landing on his back. While he lay there bleeding, the hotel's owner was just metres away, eating and drinking beer, paying no attention.

In his last post on Facebook before leaving Gaza, Mohammed wrote a message to his mother. But it could have been written by any other youth in Gaza:

'Dear Mother, I can't bear the pain of leaving you and making you worried about me day and night. But Mother, I've graduated from university, and I have no job . . . I have no future here and there is no light at the end of the tunnel. Gaza is so dark; life seems to be slow death. I don't seek to travel to find joy or happiness; I'm going because I can't forgive myself for being twenty-five and still taking pocket money from my father. I just want to have a decent job. I'm fleeing Gaza because I'm hopeless and helpless.'

He continued: 'I heard a song once that said I shouldn't feel humiliated when I am in my homeland. But what can be more humiliating than this life? Please forgive me for going far away to try my luck at finding a better life. But I will lose nothing except your smile. Pray for me. I love you so much.'

Mohammed called Gaza the 'grave of dreams'. Luck was his only hope. His story is the story of many and will be the story for many more unless the so-called 'international community' acts on its empty promises of humanity.

Issam worked as a WANN project manager in Gaza before becoming a professional journalist, working for both the Associated Press and Al Jazeera. After receiving death threats, Issam, his wife and his young daughter managed to get to Egypt. In the autumn of 2024, his wife, Farah (also a WANN writer and staffer), travelled to the UK for a scholarship. Issam and their daughter Sarah hope to join her soon.

Jehad Shehada: a 'renaissance man'
by Raed Sadi, mentored by Pam Bailey

On 19 May 2019, Israel hosted the global singing competition Eurovision. In protest at where it would be held and the inability of Palestine to send contestants, We Are Not Numbers staged 'Gazavision'.

Jehad Shehada is the top vote-getter in the We Are Not Numbers Gazavision contest.

'Why can't I do, and focus on, both of the two things I love?' asks the 23-year-old Jehad Wajeeh Shehada. He's about to graduate from university in biomedical engineering, a top student in his field. But Jehad also loves music.

He comes from a big family of ten people – four brothers and three sisters. They live in the Zaytoun neighbourhood of Gaza City. Like the majority of Palestinians in Gaza, his financial situation is rough. Jehad could not afford college but managed to get a scholarship to study at al-Azhar University. His father works for the Palestinian Authority, and he's one of many whose salary got cut off. Jehad doesn't work either because he can't find a job.

Jehad has always known he has a good voice. Ever since he was seven years old, he would melodically recite the Quran (also known as *Tajweed* reading). But he was too shy to let anyone hear him read out loud. He struggled with shyness until the tenth grade, when he took two Quran classes. Some other boys tried to read the Quran in a *Tajweed* way but failed. That led him to decide to 'go public'.

On the first day of eleventh grade, Jehad raised his hand in class to read. Everyone was shocked, and the class became quiet. Jehad blushed, his heart skipped a beat and his legs quivered. But he was satisfied with his performance and was glad to overcome his fear. After that, Jehad became the first person in class to read the Quran, and then progressed to a stage in front of the whole school. Later, he entered the Najim al-Azhar Quran-reading contest and qualified for the finals. He took second place; it was a day to remember for the rest of his life.

When Jehad began to branch out into music, it was by listening to the iconic Syrian tenor singer Sabah Fakhri. His genre is called *Qudud Halabiya*, which literally means 'musical measures of Aleppo', a form of Syrian classical music. Jehad also listens to Umm Kulthum and Abdel Halim (both iconic Egyptian singers). He loves old-school music imbued with deep meaning. Jehad couldn't afford music classes and doesn't have a camera to film himself or a microphone to sing into. 'I use my phone, and the quality of whatever I produce is not good. That prevents me from being the best on my social media accounts.'

So he depends on 'feeding his ear' to learn and improve. He practises all the time. He listens and observes. Then he applies what he learns. 'Singing is like the English language. The more you practise, the better you get,' explains Jehad.

Many people in Gaza don't believe in the value of music and singing. They view singing as trivial and worthless. Thus, it is difficult to pursue a career in this field in Gaza. Jehad's father was, and still is, against this path for Jehad. Sometimes they stop talking to each other. His father says: 'It's not an honour when someone comes and tells me "your son is a singer".'

Yet, Jehad keeps trying to talk to his father about it. He wants his father to understand him and why he desires to sing. He understands his father's concerns, despite their sting. 'He doesn't want me to be distracted from school, especially when I've been an extraordinary student since I was young.'

Society in Gaza believes one's future is based on what is studied in college. Thus, Jehad is focusing on biomedical engineering at university and maintains a good GPA [Grade Point Average]. And he loves his studies. But he believes music can be equally as influential on the world.

'Umm Kulthum never really died. Every new generation listens to her songs and love her for them. It's like immortality, in a way,' he explains.

His role model is a physician named Dalal Abu Amneh. 'She's an artist and a doctor at the same time,' he says. 'She's Palestinian and switches between singing and medicine. And her husband supports her. That's really superb!'

And Jehad is on track to do the same. So far, he has managed to excel at both his loves: engineering and singing.

Raed endured six months of the Gaza genocide, including three months spent displaced to a tent in early 2024. Then he managed to evacuate to another country, and now shoulders the responsibility of caring for his parents and little sister. Driven by a sense of duty, he's pursuing a career in media and communications. 'The Israeli blockade aims to suffocate and silence us in Gaza, to cut us off from the world. I fight back with my pen and my microphone. I'm determined to show and tell the world what I lived, witnessed and survived.'

Tragically, Jehad says he no longer sings. 'I'm living in a tent without the most basic necessities of life: clean water, sufficient food, a job. What is there to sing about?'

Hunger 2.0: an essay on my body
(Inspired by Roxane Gay's memoir *Hunger*,
a book sent to the author in Gaza by Pam Bailey)
by Omnia Ghassan, mentored by Pam Bailey

I watched a movie once and a certain scene caught my attention, inspiring me to question everything in which I had ever believed. It was a scene in which the female lead thanked a male friend for loving her, adding how his love had taught her to love herself. That's the moment when the question popped into my head: 'Do I love myself?' At that point, I fell into an abyss.

If I could draw my Punnett inheritance square (a diagram that depicts genetic inheritance), you'd realise that my excess weight is not because I regularly devour a container of ice cream when I crave sweets at midnight. Both of my grandmothers, who were sisters, were overweight (unlike their husbands, who were brothers and stick thin). My mom and dad married and produced me. With F representing 'fat' and T standing for 'thin,' there were two possibilities for my own genetic code: FF or FT. You do the maths.

I dreaded publishing this piece for months. But everything I wanted to say made me restless. And no matter how much I pushed the thought away, the more I felt the urge to write. I don't really have to explain my obesity (a task I am tired of repeating), but I am resigned to it for the sake of this essay. I was born chubby – as most kids are. But my baby fat never went away. It's still here. Sometimes I find myself blaming my parents because it's their genes that cause me to live in a body like mine, in a world like ours.

Over and over again, I tried to convince myself that if I didn't see myself as a problem then no one else would. But it didn't work. Because it is truly the other way around.

I love me some cheesy pizzas, saucy burgers, fried rice, kimbap rolls, full-of-fat fast foods that I don't have to cook, wash dishes for or clean the kitchen after. When I try to isolate myself from these addictive comfort foods, they drag me back.

In elementary school, I was 'stocky'. Then I became outright fat as I hit puberty. Now I'm obese; I became so as I struggled to survive the stress of my *tawjihi* year. (*Tawjihi* is the final exam of high school, which determines not only whether a student will be permitted to enrol at university, but also limits their selection of majors and classes.) Yes, I love food. But I hate eating around people. It feels like they're watching me eating, measuring how much I'm stuffing into my mouth – even if they're not really watching. I hate eating in front of people because I feel like I must prove my fatness is not because of the amount of food I eat.

There are two classes with which I had a love-hate

relationship: I loved PE because it didn't require studying but hated it because I was the reason my team lost races. And I loved physics because of the numbers, equations and finding solutions but hated it after my teacher said: 'If Omnia and [thin] Mai competed in running, whose kinetic energy would be greater?' The answer: 'Omnia! Because her invariant mass is bigger.'

I was in a meeting for writers once. The host was my friend. To make new writers feel welcome, she decided we should play 'Two Truths, One Lie'. We all jotted on sticky notes and then we had to guess each person's lie. When my friend read the statement 'I love food' on one of the papers, she said jokingly: 'Omnia, did you write that?' Everyone laughed. I laughed too, but it was fake. Those words still ring in my head.

I'm overweight and I don't deny it. So, don't dare tell me 'You're not fat', thinking you're being nice. You're not! But I didn't admit I was really 'fat' until recently. Rebel Wilson's role as Fat Amy in the film *Pitch Perfect* gave me the confidence I needed to embrace myself. Explaining why she gave herself such a derogatory nickname, the character says: 'So that twig bitches like you don't do it behind my back.' It hit me to the core. I didn't start calling myself 'Fat Omnia'. But I embraced my fatness. I am fat. Obese. And I'm fine with it even if I prefer to be different. This is the reality of my body. My fat. My curves. My lovable, chubby cheeks. My non-existent thigh gap.

Often, when I'm walking on the street and see people laugh, I imagine they're laughing at me even if they're most likely not. When I see kids playing on the streets, I purposely change my route, so I don't pass them. Kids are so brutally, innocently honest. They don't hesitate to call out how fat I am: 'Dobba! Dobba! Dobba!' (Bear! Bear! Bear!). I've heard that a few times as I pass by them. I wished I could grab them by their feet and swing them over my head – like a cowboy with his rope – and fling them as far away as possible.

As I walked with a friend and her eight-year-old brother to a restaurant, he popped the question I had been expecting.

'Why are you so big?' he asked, stressing 'big' with a widened gaze.

'I eat a lot,' I replied. (I figured I might as well just say what he already thinks and be done with it.)

He nodded and then asked: 'Are you pregnant?'

His sister pinched him to get him to shut up, but he just ignored her, waiting for the answer.

'No,' I replied calmly, trying to suppress my laughter. 'Why? Does your mother look like me?'

'Oh no!' he replied, offended. 'You look like my dad!'

This is actually a funny memory. I like how I played with his questions and how nonchalantly I answered. However, this confidence is not always there.

People seem to like to discuss dieting when I'm around, as if 'need to diet' is written on my face. They share their stress about the meagre one or two extra kilos they need to lose. Seriously! I mean, look at me! That's as bad as when a girl complains about how thin she is. I'd be glad to donate some of my fat to you. But it's when I hear 'Omnia, why don't you diet?' That really gets to me. Thank you! I've never actually considered that! I don't know why it hadn't crossed my mind!

I've tried so many types of dieting. I've exercised and starved myself, or banned whole categories of food, for days – just to prove to myself and others that the problem is not simply lifestyle. Nothing works. When a friend follows the same diet I'm on with much less effort, but loses 10 kilograms a week and I barely lose half a kilogram, it is so demotivating. I went to a nutritionist once and he too was surprised I didn't lose the predicted kilograms.

I love walking. I walk about three kilometres or more nearly every day. It makes me feel alive, even light. I love jumping rope too, and I do it with my niece. But my legs cramp when I jog; my calves feel like they are being hit with iron bars.

I was a member of a Facebook group for writers a few years ago, through which I made several online friendships. I was still in a phase when I was not used to sharing personal photos. But I participated in many events in which group pictures were taken and I freely shared them. One time, one of my new writer friends asked: 'So, which one is you?'

'Which one do you think?'

He started guessing. He picked every girl in the picture except me. When I was the only one left, he said: 'Don't tell me you're the girl with chubby cheeks?'

BLOCK!

I've been told it will be hard to get a job if I don't lose weight. A few months back, I applied to a project for writers and readers and I was eager to participate. I made it as far as the interview. But as I entered, the interviewers stared at me from head to toe. Suppressed disgust was apparent on their faces. I immediately knew it would be a 'no', regardless of how good my answers were. And I was right.

I've also been told I wouldn't find a husband. I was with a thin friend once when she was stopped by a woman wanting her number and address so she could ask for her hand in marriage for her son. She barely glanced at me. I thought: *A rotten apple keeps eaters away. Only sleek, firm apples attract them.* I am a rotten apple.

I was told by thin friends that 'it's OK to be fat. I feel fat too.' But they aren't even close. I am fat, but I feel and am lively, active and energetic; unlike anything people assume when they judge my body.

If you never hated shopping because you know you won't find anything that fits or looks good because 'plus' sizes aren't stylish, then you don't know how it feels to be fat. If you've never been told by countless relatives that 'you'd be pretty if you lost weight', then you don't know how it feels to be fat. If your friends haven't told you to stay the way you are because they can't imagine you thin, then you don't know how it feels to be fat. If your big behind doesn't fit into swings and slides that your childish soul yearns to ride, then you don't know how it feels to be fat.

If people don't blame every possible pain you feel on your weight, then you don't know how it feels to be fat. If taxi passengers never eye you as if they are thinking: *Oh God! Why does she have to sit here!*, then you don't know how it feels to be fat. If you never compared yourself to another obese person and try to determine who is fatter, then you simply don't know how it feels to be fat. You just don't. And never will.

I eat because I love food. I eat because gaining weight is so much easier than losing it. I eat because I yearn for someone who doesn't care about looks. I've always day-dreamed about being in the company of a person who makes me feel beautiful. I do believe such a person exists and would help me love myself. Then I think, *would I always have to feel grateful to him for having enough guts to ignore the opinions of others?*

This is my body. And now that I wrote this, I feel naked on a stage in front of thousands of people. But I am more than my body. I am more than anything you assume of me before getting to know me well. Still, I wish I will someday become as healthy-looking and fit as I want to be, especially since diabetes runs on both sides of my family. I wish I will feel free enough to stop wearing my black cloak because it covers every inch of my body and makes me feel thin. I hope I will feel comfortable wearing skirts, jeans, blouses and dresses and walk publicly without anyone piercing me with judgement in their eyes.

I know I'm worth it. I know I deserve everything to which I aspire and more. But . . . do you?

CHAPTER SIX
2020

How does it feel?
by Yara Jouda

There is a virus invader,
infecting,
killing,
widely spreading.
With an unknown creator
and a diabolical mission:
kill the most vulnerable,
spread fear in my wake,
and impose a siege on the free.

How does it feel,
forced to stay at home?
Separated from friends and family?
Seeing only your own backyard?

That has been our life
for fourteen years.
We live in a little strip:
just 40 kilometres long.
We too can't leave.
Many of us have never even *seen* a plane
(unless you count war planes).
Comfort? We don't really know

what that feels like.
We're survivors of three wars
and bombs after.
Youth are at risk as much as the old.
Strong or weak, no difference.

Covid is a disease, so it's 'non-political'.
Outrage is universal.
But it's a shame,
because while every country is helping one another,
we have faced the same for years.
Killed by the same killer, over and over.
The response: silence and indifference.

Has the pandemic made the world like Gaza?
by Aya Alghazzawi, mentored by Bridget Smith

8 a.m. I start my day feeding my four kittens and their mommy, Semsem. They are growing bigger and more energetic. My parents think I should gift them to people. But having a pet is a luxury in Gaza, with many barely able to provide food for their families these days. And meanwhile, other kittens are on their way. Semsem is pregnant for a second time!

I eat breakfast with my family and scroll through the Facebook news feed on my phone for the latest updates on Covid. The number of active cases is rapidly escalating in Gaza. The Ministry of Health is warning that the current upward trend in infections could mean the pandemic will veer out of control here, like elsewhere. We must all stay home. The coronavirus is another siege, a lockdown inside another, much longer-running lockdown.

Since I have a smartphone, Mom asks me continuously for news about the virus. I find it ironic that we are finally stressed about something other than Israeli assaults! Many Gazans have begun to think that the pandemic has thrown the rest of the world into the same boat with us. At first, paradoxically, it seemed like Gaza was protected from the virus by the fortress that is the fourteen-year Israeli-imposed siege. The restriction on our movement has prevented most people from entering Gaza for years now. However, although the government took extraordinary measures to test and quarantine the few who were allowed to enter, we knew 'community spread' was inevitable.

But are we really seeking a shared humanity in illness and vulnerability? Is the coronavirus the great leveller? Is the world the same as us now?

2 p.m. Everybody in my home is sweating. We are gloomy and fatigued. Our spirits are flagging. Our roof is a magnet for the Sun's heat, and the wind feels like an inferno outside our windows. It is the hottest month of the year. The weather broadcast says Palestine hasn't had a season this hot for 118 years. Nobody can run our fans, though, because the only power plant in Gaza has shut down, as it does periodically. (In fact, I can't recall when it was fully operational.) We change our clothes repeatedly, trying not to think of doing laundry. We all dream of having a shower, but our water tanks have been empty for three days. (In Gaza, most people store water in tanks on their roofs, using mirrors and the sunshine to warm it for bathing and dishes. The water is pumped from a spigot in the basement to the tanks when there is electricity.)

An hour later, my dad finally goes downstairs and carries buckets of water up. He toils up and down many times to procure sufficient water. We must, he says, use it only for necessary things like doing the dishes and using the bathroom.

4 p.m. We all head to the living room. We leave our bedrooms because the windows look over our neighbours' inner area and they are talking loudly; we can hear every word. This is common in the Gaza ghetto, where 2 million souls are concentrated on to 345 square kilometres. Privacy barely exists. Everyone knows everyone else's stories.

'Look! Employees are queuing in front of ATMs for their salaries. Aren't they afraid of contracting the virus?' my sister asks.

'They have kids to feed. They need the money,' my brother responds. 'What choice do they have?'

'They are paid only 50 per cent of their salaries anyway,' my sister sighs.

7 p.m. Piles of clothes need washing. We are running out of bread. There is supposed to be four hours of electricity every day, but we fall short. It's extremely hot in here. Our bodies are on fire. We wave plastic plates like fans to create a puff of air. It will soon be dark. Oh, God, grant us patience. The young ones start complaining.

9 p.m. The children sleep on the floor to cool off. We turn on the LED lights, which are a safe alternative to the candles that too often cause fires. Houses have burnt down and whole families have died because of them. Mom asks me to call my brother Muhannad in Algeria to check on him. 'My battery is almost dead. I'll call him tomorrow,' I answer.

10.10 p.m. The electricity is ON! Everyone rushes

to plug in appliances and charge phones. Mom turns on the washing machine and then hurries to the flour container and starts kneading dough for our bread. We help her with baking and later with packing the bread in bags. When all is done, I surf the internet. Breaking news reads: 'Three siblings in Nuseirat camp die as a candle burns their home.' I gasp at Gaza's fresh tragedy.

11.30 p.m. I rest my head on my pillow, thinking of my cat and her little babies, the horrible Nuseirat accident and my brother, who I long to call. That question jumps into my head again: 'Can the suffering of the world be equated with ours?' My mind responds with an emphatic *hell no!*

Aya married shortly before the genocide began and was displaced to Khan Younis after everything she owned was destroyed. When asked how she is faring, she responded: 'I find this question very difficult to answer. I have lost the language to put it into words.'

One girl's joust with depression
by Asmaa Tayeh, mentored by Pam Bailey

For twenty-four years, I have lived through many events that justify feelings of sadness, anger and depression – from ongoing Israeli attacks to the ever-present sound of Israeli drones, to the inability to travel out of this biggest open-air prison, to the lack of jobs. But talking about all of that and the effect on our mental health is not easy. Our brains are somehow programmed to think: *We are heroes and can endure and fight against anything.* Well, for me, that is not the case!

Our supporters overseas expect us to be strong, always ready to resist. And our own culture and religion dictate the same – that we should be steadfast and never give up. This means we fear being judged as weak and vulnerable if we say we are depressed or pessimistic. Plus, every one of the 2 million people living in this 365-square-kilometre area faces almost the same challenges, so we don't have much patience for others' issues; we all need help. I believe so many of us need help so badly that we no longer can help each other.

I work hard to find ways to avoid becoming a victim of deep depression. I seek out new experiences (although the options are a bit limited here) and push myself to share my thoughts and feelings with friends. I even try sleeping more than usual in a desperate attempt to stop overthinking, and sometimes force myself to join activities with new people so I am too busy to dwell on the fact that I am not fine. Recently, to escape depression, I tried sleeping *less* and buried myself in loads of work. But deep inside, the depression monster lurks. I am saying that in public and it does not mean I am weak or pathetic. I believe it means I'm human. A human who is sick and tired of always acting strong.

I once organised an activity I called 'Depression solutions' as part of the meetings we call 'The Circle' at We Are Not Numbers. At each circle, a volunteer writer chooses a controversial topic to discuss with the others. I led a discussion on how all of us deal with depression so we could learn from each other. I managed to get most of the participants out of their comfort zones by making them talk about their private struggles. Just being able to talk and having someone willingly listen was stress-releasing.

But at the same time, these discussions made me realise once again that facing depression in Gaza is not easy. Most of us simply don't know what normal is any more. Our lives as Palestinians have never been normal anyway! It's become so difficult to understand people and hack their personalities and reactions. And this is what has made it so hard for me to be fine and happy during the last couple of months. My relationships with everyone around me seem complicated; I must be careful about how to say things or act. As a result, I find it hard to be myself, because I am focusing on being careful, so I do not hurt people around me. I want to be the nice, helpful person in the room who allows others to feel safe to be themselves but end up not feeling safe myself. I wish we could all do that for each other, so we heal each other's wounds.

Sometimes people search for a good listener, whether they know the person or not. That is exactly what happens to me. People I barely know unburden themselves and ask for advice, then say: 'I don't know why I am sharing that, but I thought you would understand me.' Well, I love that! But then I end up worrying about them and that makes me even more depressed.

Our parents often fight depression by ignoring it and even believing it doesn't exist. In fact, this is one of the biggest problems faced by Gazan youths: the wide gap between parents and children. Parents grew up in a better time, when they could travel and find work more easily. So, when we admit to feeling depressed, some parents say: 'You're exaggerating! If you were really depressed, you wouldn't be able to leave your bed for days! Just be an adult and go on!'

Even the word 'depression' evokes a different reaction inside and out of Gaza. I hear that out of Gaza, if you say you're depressed, the people around you are immediately concerned. But here, people often joke about it or compare your circumstances to others to show that you don't have the right to be depressed. Being depressed here is like being thirsty; everyone is!

Actually, stories of youths committing suicide because of depression (no matter what the reason behind it) seem almost common and expected now.

People's reactions are like this:

A: 'Mohammed fought depression before he hung himself.'

B: 'Oh really? May he rest in peace.'

And life goes on.

As the operations manager and a long-time writer for We Are Not Numbers, I've had the opportunity at least fifteen times to represent Gazan youth with the media and on webinars. Many NGOs now see us as a go-to source for the 'youth perspective'. I find myself ending my remarks with: 'I am really sorry for all the negativity. I hope soon you will invite me again and I will have stories of happiness and success to share.'

Last year, members of the USA Palestine Mental Health Network met a number of us from We Are Not Numbers in Gaza and I told them how depression affects our ability to write and be productive. We don't seek help from professionals here because of the stigma associated with it. If it is known that you are seeing a psychotherapist, you are labelled crazy or mentally 'slow'! In response, they offered online sessions. But I could not bring myself to take advantage of them. I simply can't convince myself that it will help, especially when the therapist can't really understand what we Palestinians in Gaza live every day.

The Gaza Strip is like one big, crowded community. If you want to be alone with your misery, it's almost impossible. Your family want to take you to visit relatives, or your relatives visit you. If you're fortunate enough to have a job, your co-workers scold you if you're silent at your desk. Your friends are trying to escape depression themselves, so they don't want you to be 'the negative one'. You can almost never say no to social activities because that's seen as disrespectful in our society.

A friend finally decided to overcome the stigma and seek help. His first attempt was when a manager of a mental health centre offered sessions for free. But the manager never showed up for four appointments over two weeks. He later justified his lack of follow-through by saying: 'I am busy with some paid programmes.' The second attempt was with a private therapist who he liked, but he couldn't afford more than three visits. And that was the end of that.

As devout Muslims, we try to follow Islam's rules in every aspect of our lives. Most people believe faith alone will stave off depression. And it does help to believe in God and His plans for us. But sometimes we need more than that. We need to learn how to deal with uncertainty. We need to know how to find hope even in the darkest times. We need to learn how to be productive despite our worsening life circumstances.

The reality is this: depression is even more frightening than Israeli forces. I want NGOs to fight it with us. We have lost so much since Israel was created on our land in 1948, and the only power we have right now – a hopeful generation – could be lost soon.

After leaving Gaza briefly for Turkey, where she and her mother received much-needed medical treatment, Asmaa returned to Gaza. However, they both need further treatment, and are anxious to leave Gaza as soon as the border opens. 'The pollution from the daily air strikes and wood fires has been very bad for my lungs,' she explains. Asmaa has been forced to leave her home in Jabalia camp five times to date.

My hair is my identity
by Raed Sadi, mentored by Pam Bailey

I've always wanted to grow my hair long, but my father, because of social expectations, thinks it's inappropriate for a guy. When I was young, my hair was thick, soft and straight. But because of Gaza's polluted, salty water, it started to dry out and curl. I transformed from the kid with nice hair to the guy with unruly, almost scary-looking hair; kids stared when they saw me on the street. 'The one with hair' is who I am. I even sport a small hair bun now, although I untie it when I go out, simply because Gaza society isn't ready for that.

Recently, I let it grow even longer and I justified it to my father by warning that I might catch the coronavirus at a barbershop. Of course, that's a lie; I've only gone to a barbershop twice since I returned to Gaza from the United States on 25 December 2016. But it's my identity now: the dude with long, black hair.

I remember both times at the barber very well. The first was when I had just returned to Gaza. My hair was long because during my five months in the US, I hadn't cut my hair (except some trimming I did myself). My dad couldn't tolerate it, so sent me straight to have a haircut the next day. The second time was in 2019. I cut my hair at home myself, and I mistakenly shortened it too much in the back because I could not see very well, so I needed a professional barber to 'fix' it.

Almost no one in Gaza cuts their hair at home. Haircuts are very cheap in Gaza, unlike in the US. Children can get a haircut for a dollar (£0.75), and teenagers pay $2. As for men, they can get professional haircuts for less than $3. Of course, for females, the prices are higher, as is almost everything else, like clothing.

Another reason people in Gaza don't cut their hair themselves is the cost of buying a hair clipper, and the electricity needed for the types that do the best job. Gaza's constant power outages force us to prioritise housework and other vital tasks when we're fortunate enough to have electricity. And then there's the need to learn how to cut hair, particularly your own. Talking from experience, I can say it's not so easy!

But I decided to try, and I've become better over time. Almost no one can tell I do it myself. Yet I also love my hair when it's messy. To me, it is not just hair; it is a part of who I am as a person. This wild, black hair is my Arab identity. The same is true for my father. He was called 'the Korean guy' in his youth because of his distinctive hair.

The first time I linked my hair with my identity was in May 2019, when We Are Not Numbers organised its singing contest Gazavision. My fellow writer Omnia Ghassan told me she loved my messy hair, or maybe I should say my 'riot' hair. Other people had probably said that before, but it seemed different that day. A huge event like Gazavision is unusual in Gaza, and singing isn't common either. It was unique, and I felt unique with my long, messy black hair. I took a selfie on that day with my friend's iPhone. It is one of my favourite selfies of all time, and it is hanging on the wall at WANN's office.

Still, not all is good with my hair. I am twenty-two and my hair is already turning grey. It started when I was eighteen. I was a senior in high school, the *tawjihi* year that determines what university you can attend and what you can study. Due to the huge pressure, I think, the first grey hair showed up. After four years of university, you can imagine how full of grey my head is now! I hated it at first, but now I love it. I've started to accept it, since many people told me grey hair means wisdom; whether it's true or not, it makes me feel sort of distinctive.

So many young people get grey hair here, though, so it won't be true for long. There may be genetic reasons, but it's different in Gaza. I believe the main reason people grey early here is fear and stress. It's partially from the repeated, brutal Israeli wars on Gaza. But there is so much more feeding the fear. Most college students fear unemployment after they graduate, for instance. I was, and still partially am, one of those people. (I am employed only part-time by We Are Not Numbers.)

Listing all the reasons why we are depressed and turning grey here would require a book. Maybe it's one that should be written; maybe these simple stories of fear and grey hair will penetrate more than politics can.

How Gaza inspired me to be a 'surgeon' for historic buildings
by Eman Shawwa, mentored by Mazin Qumsiyeh

When I was a child walking to elementary school, I'd pass by massive, castle-like buildings in the old part of Gaza City. They fascinated me because they were so different from the buildings around my home.

One day, I asked my mom why they were so different. 'They were built a long time before our home,' she said simply. I wasn't satisfied. 'But Grandpa's house was built before ours, and it is in our same style. Why is that?!'

Being a curious girl, I continued with my 'why and how' questions. I wouldn't stop until I understood. My mom had no other choice but to teach me a bit about Gaza's architectural history, including how buildings differed from one era to another.

As expected, it was difficult for a little girl to understand the new words. My mom tried using metaphors so I could grasp new ideas. 'Gaza is like a human being, a person. A person begins small, then grows up over time to become old. It's sort of the same with buildings; they are "born" in one form, but their size and condition changes with time, until they are old and worn.'

For me, that was clearer and more convincing!

My fascination with historical, castle-like buildings grew.

I was overwhelmed with joy whenever my class went on a school trip to visit these vestiges of our history. These school trips offered rare opportunities to walk inside the buildings and get to know them more intimately. The building that most fascinated me as a child was Qasr al-Basha, which local legend says was built by the thirteenth-century Mamluk sultan Baybars for a Gazan woman whom he fell in love with and married. Romantic, right?

While I was flipping through TV channels one day, I stumbled upon a documentary explaining how archaeologists study ancient buildings and try to prevent them from collapsing or eroding away. It seemed to me that these archaeologists were like surgeons, trying to prolong the lives of their elderly patients. They clean the worn stones and inject substances that prevent corrosion. The buildings embody the world's history and so we must care for them.

I couldn't stop wondering why I didn't see similar methods used to protect and preserve the historic buildings in Gaza City. As the days passed, I learned that in Gaza, it's the architects who care for old buildings. (I've since discovered that in more well-resourced countries, preservation is the province of specialists called conservators, with architects designing new or remodelled buildings.) I decided to become what I like to think of as a 'surgeon for historical buildings'.

So I started my studies at the Islamic University of Gaza (IUG) in 2008 and I became an architectural engineer. While studying, I enrolled in every programme and organisation I could that was relevant to the preservation of Gaza's architectural heritage. One of these is IWAN, a centre at IUG that works to restore and preserve Gaza's historic urban sites, trains professionals in the art and educates the public. As a member of the team there, I collected social and economic data for residents living in historic buildings, like the number of family members and their employment status. When donor funds become available for renovation, we prioritise by need and the condition of the building.

There are so many buildings falling down, with the walls eroding due to moisture – threatening to make their residents homeless with no protection from the cold of winter and the searing summers. I see now the need to spread awareness of the value of these structures to our heritage and what we can do, as a people, to save them.

To be fair, there are quite a lot of renovated residential buildings, but sadly, the techniques have not always made them better; instead, sometimes erosion of the stone accelerates. Other buildings have been demolished by their owners who are unaware of, or don't care about, their historic value. They do this to replace them with bigger houses that can accommodate a family's expansion in one of the most densely populated places on Earth. Two million people live on 365 square kilometres. That's 5,479 people per square kilometre.

Our government is too poor to offer any financial support to owners of historic buildings. Something else I came to realise is that there is not enough experience in the field of architectural heritage preservation in Gaza. With so many life-or-death crises here, protecting buildings always ends up at the bottom of the government's priority list.

It's also important to note that Gaza's ancient buildings and heritage suffer first and foremost due to the Israeli blockade. The blockade prevents many construction materials from entering the Strip and any that make it in are immediately used to rebuild houses and essential public buildings destroyed by the Israelis' relentless bombing. The siege is also the main obstacle to communicating and collaborating with any international experts and organisations.

Sometimes I wonder how close we are to losing the architectural heritage of Gaza. If still-living souls, crying out from Gaza to the outside world, are barely heard, how will ancient stones fare any better before they erode away, taking with them the history of a city and a people? Will anybody hear their silent cries before it is too late?

If you want to erase a nation, start with its history. Gaza City's history is a big part of the history of Palestine, the Fertile Crescent and the Holy Land. We all need to care because it is a part of our human history.

Eman remains in Gaza, and has been forced to relocate three times. She had been pursuing her master's degree in business administration before the genocide began, but has been unable to

complete her thesis (on entrepreneurship and the sustainability of startups in the Gaza Strip) due to the internet blackouts. She hasn't felt safe enough to venture out to see what has happened to the historic buildings she loves so much, but she is aware of the statistics: 'More than 60 per cent of our buildings here have been destroyed. The rest are damaged to some degree.'

The nightmare that is online shopping (in Gaza)
by Akram Abunahla, mentored by Greta Berlin

Since 2010, consumers around the world increasingly shop online. Whether we want to replace our weary guitar strings, try new flavours of coffee or snag the current bestselling books, online shopping is now the go-to option. Simply surf, click and get it delivered.

Not for us, though. Living in Gaza means nothing is easy and online shopping is no exception. Here are just a few examples of what we must tolerate to place and receive an order.

I'm in love with traditional divine music. My love for music led me to become obsessed with collecting my own set of CDs. (Even now, with Spotify, I still have a fondness for old-fashioned CDs. One of my favourite performers is Sami Yusuf, and his albums are packaged with booklets that describe the lyrics. Sometimes, a rosary is included. So I often choose to support my favourite artists by purchasing the 'real thing'.) Since his albums aren't available in retail stores in Gaza, I decided to order Yusuf's *The Centre* album from his official online store.

The online transaction was processed flawlessly and I received a confirmation email saying my delivery should take no longer than two weeks. I waited and waited, but it never arrived. I heard from other fans around the world that they received their copies on time. How frustrating! It never did arrive; it was no match for the Israeli blockade. On the bright side, I managed to get a refund after several weeks.

In 2014, I decided to study English language and literature at al-Azhar University of Gaza. That major requires students to read many literary works (such as novels and poetry) not available in our local bookstores and libraries. After my experience two years before, I wasn't eager to try online shopping again, but I was desperate.

This time, I decided to spend £45 of my savings on books. Via Amazon, I ordered *Merriam-Webster's Advanced Learner's English Dictionary*, *The Complete Works of Shakespeare*, *Longman Pocket Phrasal Verbs Dictionary* and *Merriam-Webster's Vocabulary Builder*. On the site, I was asked for my shipping and payment details, and I used my dad's credit card. Although Palestine was listed in the country list, many of my friends who had already purchased from Amazon recommended selecting Israel for the shipping country and adding Palestine next to the city.

As a Palestinian, I was insulted, but I took their advice because I needed the books. I completed the order. After forty days of anxious waiting, I received a text message while I was asleep. It was from the post office, informing me my package had arrived. I could not believe my eyes! I had just received my first package ever! I rushed out of bed and grabbed a taxi. I didn't wait to wash my face or eat breakfast. I was even still wearing my pyjamas.

I sat in the back seat, imagining how my package would look. I entered the Rafah post office with a wide smile on my face, saying 'hello' to everyone. I showed the post office employee the text message. He asked for my mobile number and ID card and asked me to have a seat while he retrieved the package.

The package was big and was sealed with 'Amazon Prime' tape. I slipped out the door and, without thinking, ripped open the package. I couldn't wait. I touched the book covers gently with my fingertips. I stared at the package for a minute or two and then held it close to my chest and went home. When I arrived, the first thing I did was put the books on my empty bookshelf and pledged to fill it soon. I stored the now-empty box under my bed. And it's been there ever since. (I keep all the boxes I receive; each arrival is so special.)

Receiving my order came as a relief after the first disappointing experience. Some of the book covers were slightly damaged, but I could live with that; to receive slightly damaged books is better than not receiving them.

Then I heard about a Palestinian company specialising in logistics and mail service that is contracting with the Ministry of Telecommunications and Information Technology to manage overseas packages for a small fee (£0.75). Once a package clears customs (a process in which your items could be seized or partially damaged or even destroyed), it informs you by SMS to pick up your package. I decided to give it a try.

One of my work colleagues asked me to purchase the

Game of Thrones book set for him, and this time the experience was horrible. We waited over forty days, but the order never arrived. The shipping information I received showed that the item was on its way. Since our order was covered by Amazon's guarantee (receive your order in time or your money back), we were eligible for a refund, but, of course, we really wanted the books. They never came.

A few months later, Seyyed Hossein Nasr published his long-awaited work *The Study Quran* (a translation and study version of the holy book) and I really wanted it. Again, I purchased it from Amazon and after waiting a month, the book never arrived. I contacted Amazon customer support, which offered me two options: get a refund or request a replacement. As I desperately wanted the book, I went with the second option.

Amazon support was very helpful; not only did it ship the book using the fastest available method, DHL Express, it also refunded the shipping costs, so the book was sent for free. Using DHL Express meant I could track the package. This information revealed why I didn't receive my previous orders. They were stuck in Ashdod waiting for customs clearance. I contacted Amazon support again. The staff recommended I contact DHL Express and gave me the contact information.

DHL's answer: 'Only official documents, such as IDs, birth certificates and passports, are allowed to be shipped into Gaza using our service.' If we wanted books, we were out of luck. I was shocked. On the other hand, Israeli settlers, who live on illegally seized Palestinian land, receive their packages on time, often in less than a week! More importantly, they don't have to select Palestine or any other country when entering their shipping details and their packages don't get damaged or opened.

We, however, have no control over our packages, since they arrive at the port of Ashdod in Israel, and are delayed, sometimes for over a year, by the Israeli occupation.

What hurts me the most is that Palestine is often not found in the country list on online stores.

Even if it is, we Palestinians need to select Israel as our shipping address, otherwise we won't receive our packages. Israel is busy erasing us, even when we order online.

I have friends all over the world who receive their orders in a timely manner. Why does it have to be different for us? The Israeli occupation has deprived me of a basic human right: to read a book I can hold in my hand.

Yes, we can read e-books, but I want to fill my bookcase with books I can touch, smell and open. I have always wanted to idly flip through the pages of the books I yearn to own.

Akram now lives in Egypt. His family relocated before him; Akram says he didn't want to leave Gaza. 'But I had no choice except to finally follow them. We lost both our apartment in Gaza City and our small house in Rafah. There was nothing left.' He earns some income by teaching English phonetics and phonology to students from Murcia, Spain.

Long live sunny Friday mornings
by Butien Riman, mentored by Pam Bailey

I woke up with a sense of anticipation. Today is Friday and my family will go to the beach – our 'jewel' and the one place we can all go to escape.

I head to the kitchen to prepare some food to take with my two sisters and mum. We brew some mint tea and assemble sandwiches with our favourite fillings: za'atar and cheese. Then we add them to a basket with some oranges and water bottles. The sea is three kilometres from our home, about a fifteen-minute drive. We wedge ourselves into our family car – ten years old, but my dad has managed to keep it in mint shape. Today, all seven of us are crammed in – my dad driving, my fifteen-year-old brother on my mum's legs up front, and the rest of us wedged in the back.

I stick my head out the window, letting the wind whip into my face and breathing the scent of the orange and guava orchards. The citrusy smell is subtle at first but deepens as we drive. The oranges are so large they seem almost ready to drop. As my youngest brother turns the music up, the party in the back seat begins. It's the popular Lebanese singer Nassif Zeytoun and the song is 'Takke'. It's frequently played at weddings, so dancing is our immediate response. We may be crowded, but we can wave our arms and shimmy! My father watches us through the rear-view mirror, joining in by moving his eyebrows and sometimes waving one of his hands.

As we draw closer to the coast, we must make what has become a controversial decision in our family. What direction should we go to get to the beach: left or right? We all want a spot far away from the tents under which people gather, so we can have a clear view of the sea. But we disagree on the best place for that. Since I am the oldest of the bunch, I speak up: 'Baba, go right! Allah will grant us the privilege of being with the right people.' Everyone goes along, saying: 'Amen!' But my dad surprises us all and turns left. We burst into laughter because he never takes my suggestions seriously.

We finally get to the seaside. As the car engine stops, we leap out of the car, weighed down with our bags, and race towards the beach in bare feet. I couldn't see anything but the colourful fishermen's boats, resting like weary travellers, and the endless turquoise sea. My parents stretch out on the golden beach to soak up the sun. My siblings and I race around, collecting seashells. We end up standing facing the water and screaming as loud as we can until our throats are sore.

We go back to our spot to recharge and prepare for the most amusing part of the day: a football match. My parents are the goalkeepers, and the rest of us divide into offence and defence. We play for fun; my father and brothers aren't big football fans. Time flies quickly, so my mother surprises all of us when she announces there are only two hours left to get ready for *Jummah* (Friday) prayer. We trudge back to the car after the match is over. On the way home, as we pass through the main checkpoint and show our IDs, we play the song 'Ya Rabbi Ehmi el-Quds' (Oh my Lord, save al-Aqsa Mosque).

The scene I just described took place earlier this year, during our winter. It would be impossible during the summer holiday, when the beach is packed with Gazan families. Gazan women usually chit-chat while watching their kids. Only occasionally will you see a woman swimming, or a group of young women splashing in the waves where it's shallow. Here in Gaza, women try to engage in their favourite activities in a way that doesn't disrespect our religion's norms and traditions. Some women swim by having their men form a circle around them with their bodies, so they have some privacy. Of course, they still wear their long *abayas* (cloaks), which stick to their bodies when wet. Women who can afford £75–£200 rent a private chalet with a pool, so they can swim freely, wearing whatever they want, without worrying about looks from men outside of the family.

The other complication of swimming in Gaza is the increasing pollution in our sea, due to the lack of equipment and fuel needed for proper waste treatment. The al-Mezan Centre for Human Rights reports that levels of raw sewage in the sea have soared by 73 per cent, which means those who can't afford private pools are at risk of disease.

But we Gazans are sons and daughters of the sea. Enjoying it to the full extent is our birthright.

Butien remains in Gaza and estimates that her family have had to relocate eight or nine times. 'We've lost count,' she says. While she used to have a decent job teaching English online to people in Bahrain and Saudi Arabia, the lack of reliable access to internet and the constant need to move have made that work impossible.

CHAPTER SEVEN
2021

A degree in surviving assaults
by Basman Derawi, mentored by Pam Bailey

If there were a degree bestowed
for surviving armed assaults,
I would have earned it 'with honours',
magna cum laude.
I am living through my fourth now,
although I'm not sure if
I will live for graduation.

If you test me, I bet I'd ace the exam:
I can tell the difference between
the voice of an F-16, F-35 and Apache helicopter.
I can immediately detect
whether a sound is
the shelling of tanks
or bombing from airplanes.

But with my degree has come
different types of syndromes:
phobia of the night,
hypersensitivity to the sound
of moving chairs
(or really any banging object),
insomnia from anticipating death.

I have also learned a few truths.
First: the world is hypocritical,
yet is full of hidden gems;
good people willing to speak out.
Second: actual death is when you don't
stand up for what is right.
And third: no matter what,
Palestine will always be my home.

Love is more than a family name
by Orjwan Shurrab, mentored by Pam Bailey

I was born in Gaza into a family divided by divorce and a father who had never wanted a daughter, only sons. My only way of escaping this reality was to dream. I dreamt of creating my own family even before I was old enough to understand what marriage was. I dreamt of having my own kids and doing it the 'right' way before I learned how babies were created. I dreamt of being a mother even though I didn't know how to raise a child.

I believed in myself. I knew I would be able to give another human being what I didn't have. Imagining being able to give a child what I longed for became a kind of therapy.

A few years ago, I finally met a man who believed in me as much as I believed in myself, and marriage allowed me to be independent of my father. (A fact of life about life in Gaza: females remain under the 'supervision' to some extent of the males in their family until they marry.)

But completing the rest of my dream – giving birth to my own child – was harder than I realised it would be. I tried and tried to get pregnant, and then when I did, I suffered two miscarriages. A doctor finally discovered I have too much TSH hormone. With the help of medication,

I became pregnant again three months later, but had to stay in bed for four months to guard against another miscarriage. I was so very afraid of losing this baby like the other ones! The days seemed very long.

And then, finally, my dream came true. On 9 February, I gave birth to a baby girl. Yes, a girl! While many people in my society prefer their first child to be a boy, which usually means greater financial support for the family and a legacy for their name, I was filled with joy. This meant I could give a young girl what every female deserves and should have in any society: the opportunity to develop to her full potential. And that's not easy in Gaza.

My father used to say that I didn't deserve his family name: Shurrab. So, when my husband Mohammed suggested we name our first baby Orjwan, I was so very happy. It showed how much he loves and appreciates having me in his life.

But naming our daughter after me is significant in another way. It is a type of catharsis. It is almost like giving birth to a new Orjwan, a version who will have a different life, a girl whose father will always be proud of her, and who will always know (because we will show her) that she's more valuable than a family name!

Outsiders may not know that Gaza is divided according to one's status as either an original Gazan (meaning your ancestors were originally from the Gaza Strip) or a 'refugee' (meaning your grandparents were forced to flee to Gaza in 1948, when Israel was first created). While some people who live here don't care which you are, others – like my father – look down on the refugees. The first comment he uttered upon hearing someone's name was either 'S/he is a Gazan; good!' or 'He is a refugee. Bad enough!'

When I chose Mohammed to marry, my father declared it another reason to consider me a failure. You can guess why! I'm a native-born Gazan. Mohammed is a refugee. His family originally came from Jaffa and now live in Khan Younis. Some of them were displaced to Jordan as well. And now my little Orjwan will hold the name of a family who loves her more than mine ever has, a refugee family.

To my baby girl
Dear angel, I drew pictures of you in my mind before you were even conceived. Holding you in my arms and looking into your eyes is my greatest joy. I already know that my greatest achievement in life is giving you a family who will always love you. Before you were born, I reviewed in my mind every night a list of things I should do and not do to make you happy. Number one was to give you a caring father.

My little Orjwan, be brave but patient, outspoken but kind, strong but compassionate. Be yourself. Love yourself as much as we love you! Trust yourself and know that nothing will defeat you except yourself.

Your parents promise that neither Gaza's situation nor people's attitudes will stop us from supporting you to achieve whatever you dream of.

The donkey carts of Gaza
by Hassan Alalami, mentored by Lynn Huber

Donkey carts may be slow, but they are cheap and essential for survival in this part of the world.

They are found everywhere in Gaza. You can't go a single day without coming across one, or at least notice a hint on the ground telling you that one has recently passed by. And, if you're a homebody and don't get out much, don't worry! You'll surely hear them!

Donkey carts serve several purposes. First, and perhaps most important: basic municipal services, such as trash collection. The lack of motorised vehicles, spare parts and fuel has forced many municipalities to deploy donkey carts to help collect the tons of solid waste produced daily in Gaza. The workers begin before dawn and by the time daylight arrives, the drivers' megaphone-enhanced announcements echo in the streets. By noon they are done with the collection of all the garbage they can find.

Donkey carts also have become a fixture in the Gazan landscape as they haul tanks used to water the trees and flowers on the streets. Owners can also be found lined up outside the United Nations food distribution centres in Gaza, waiting to load and then deliver food rations, including sacks of rice and flour. For heavier cargo, such as steel and cement, the carts may be pulled by horses.

Donkey carts are also used as mobile markets throughout the city. Owners sell goods like fruit, vegetables and fish from them. Many Gazans buy from donkey carts to save themselves the effort of paying a visit to the market. Other carts sell swimming gear for kids near the beach.

But there is another, relatively recent additional use for donkey carts, the result of repeated attacks by the Israeli Air Force on houses, hospitals and schools. It's to remove stones and damaged steel from the Shujaiya neighbourhood east of Gaza, an area that was heavily bombed in 2014, and from the many other neighbourhoods that were targeted and destroyed by Israeli air attacks. The same necessity arose again in May 2021.

The damaged steel is reworked so that it can be sold as new building material. Stones are also recycled in inventive ways. Donkey carts do much of the work of transporting the materials, contributing to Gaza's ability to expand its port facilities with these not-so-raw materials. Some people think it's weird to still be using donkey carts in the twenty-first century. They also complain about the noise donkey carts make, particularly in the early mornings. But others view donkey carts as a wonderful and practical source of income and employment opportunities for the poverty-stricken people of the Gaza Strip.

An alternative is the tuk-tuk, a cross between a motorcycle and a mini pickup truck. The tuk-tuk is a good choice for those donkey cart owners able to make the upgrade. They are found in growing numbers in Gaza and are also used for a variety of delivery services but are not yet a real threat to the carts.

For now, the donkeys have a secure job; there is no unemployment for them!

Hassan is studying medicine in Hungary. Although his parents and siblings managed to escape to Egypt, his relatives on his mother's side were all killed during Israel's incursion into northern Gaza. His family on his father's side are still alive in Gaza.

Flashbacks of smoke and solidarity
by Hanan Abukmail, mentored by Ben Al Wardi

17 May 2021: Day 6 of the latest Israeli military attack on Gaza.

'Hanan, it's after one in the afternoon and you haven't slept since yesterday,' my sister said. I had been tossing and turning in bed for two hours. At least I tried to sleep. My sister's voice trembled with worry, and she looked at me with sorrow. She was shaken after seeing me weep when looking at photos of a young Palestinian child who lost his father. I looked into her eyes and tried to show her that I was OK, but an abrupt beep from my phone pulled me away.

It was an email from Diane Williamson, an administrator from the Durham Palestine Educational Trust in the United Kingdom, a woman I have never met in person, yet whose solidarity and strength gave me hope that we have not been forgotten.

I started to drift back asleep. I will respond once I wake up, I thought.

Smoke

Three hours later: 'Wake up! Wake up! Wake up!' The sounds of Israeli military drones, missiles and warplanes filled my room. The sound is impossible to imagine without living through it in person. I covered my ears and hunched into a small ball on the floor, reverting to a fetal position, wishing I could disappear and be reborn somewhere more peaceful, more hopeful, safer.

The scent of toxic smoke from a nearby rocket explosion filled my nostrils, burning them. I ran to the living room, where I found my brother holding his phone. *Where are the bombs? Whose home was hit this time? Any injuries? Any losses? Can you hear the cries?!!! Which sound is worse: the missiles and warplanes or the sounds of people shrieking after an attack?*

'No news yet, but it seems close by,' my brother mumbled as he approached the window to assess the devastation. I did not have his courage. I was too scared to look out the window and too scared to check the news. I could not bear to see what I could hear and smell. My mind raced and I imagined a destroyed building full of families buried alive, a deep crater on fire with mangled and disfigured cars melting under the rocket fire amid scorched streets, playgrounds and shopping centres. Breathe, Hanan, breathe. No more sleep. Who can sleep in these conditions?

Solidarity

I returned to my bed, sat down and peered at my phone as it lit up with a string of messages. It was a rescue line, pulling me out of my vortex of panic. My amazing cancer research team across Palestine, in Gaza, the West Bank and Jerusalem, sent message after message of resilience, support and prayers for our safety. I read each message carefully. I read each message twice. Every single word washed over me like magic and filled me with power.

Checkpoints, home demolitions, heavy bombardments unite us. We are one. We have one state, we are one people. Our solidarity is real.

If I die

A month earlier, on 17 April, I spent my days and nights buried in medical research, reading and drafting an article on cervical cancer awareness for the *BMC Women's Health* journal. I shared drafts and revisions with our research group, all of us so hopeful and impressed by our work together. Through this article, I hoped to save lives by educating women on early cancer screening and prevention. I am a doctor, and my purpose is to protect and save lives. Now I wondered, *will I live to celebrate the publication of our article?*

The 'If I die' scenarios haunted me many times during this attack. Still, I looked at the mirror and repeated: *I am alive. I am alive and I will live.* I was afraid and unsure, but I kept repeating it. *Hanan, you will live. Move forward, Hanan.*

Oh! I haven't responded to Diane's email yet. I stared at the three simple words in the subject line: Solidarity from Durham.

> *Just to let you know that we are thinking of you. I know from our many friends in Gaza the horror of what is happening and what a nightmare you are living through. Be at least encouraged that there are lots of people who support you in the UK and indeed in the world. We have been organising protests*

in Durham and find that people are keen to understand what is happening and are appalled by Israeli brutality. Please let me know that you and your families are safe.

Yours in solidarity,
Diane

Diane's message was a hand in my hand, interlocking Palestine with the cause of justice, freedom and humanity all around the world.

I replied to Diane: *Please pray for those alive under the rubble, pray for those injured in the hospitals, pray for the families of martyrs and injured, pray for Gaza. Please pray that the international community will WAKE UP and stop these war crimes!*

Put your hands in mine.

Hanan, who completed her medical training in Gaza, travelled to the UK before the war broke out in October 2023 to complete a postgraduate degree at Cambridge University. She is currently a member of the International Health System Research Group at the University of Cambridge and a research fellow at the London School of Hygiene and Tropical Medicine. Hanan had planned to return to Gaza after graduating from Cambridge, but the war has prevented her. Instead, she lives with the hope of being able to embrace her mother, father and siblings again, who are still in northern Gaza.

CHAPTER EIGHT

2022

My home
by Eman Alhaj Ali, mentored by Kevin Hadduck

What is home?
This place where a wall can explode,
a table fly and spin,
glass shatter faster than a flinch?

These hours
when refreshment and conversation
flash by like commercials
in a television series called War?

The cast changes in each episode.
A sister dies. A cousin disappears.
A father is killed. A brother.
A cat. A mother. A teacher.

Every hero appears just once.
The whole series may last
a season, a month, a week.
Someone else controls the schedule.

Noise of the drones disturbs our dreams.
Our beds and couches turn to rubble.
Our wedding plans morph into funerals.

Where is home?
My little sister dreams and despairs
of travelling, studying, working,
spending quiet hours.
Not counting seconds
until the next bomb explodes our walls.

Eman remains in Gaza, and her family have been forced to relocate more than seven times – 'from tents, to streets, to relatives'. Fortunately, she completed her bachelor's degree in English literature and translation before the 2023 Israeli war on Gaza began. She is a translator, storyteller and writer, with her byline appearing on a number of international websites. Reading and writing are her passions. 'Writing is the act through which I share part of my soul with the world,' she says.

Interrupted graduation
by Aseel Zeineddin, mentored by Gail Blackhall

When I woke up, I immediately thought: *What should I wear today?* The afternoon of 5 August 2022 we were to celebrate the graduation of my older sister, Safaa. After six years in medical school, she was now becoming a doctor. For years, diligent, exhausted Safaa had alternated between long hours at the hospital and nights studying weighty medical textbooks under dim lights while everyone else slept. Finally, she was ready to take the next step. I couldn't wait to applaud her proudly as she gave her speech to the doctors, parents and fellow students. I'd been excited for this day since the beginning of her last year of medical school.

I was overwhelmed with happiness as I sat looking at the pictures she had sent to us earlier in the day, when she was getting her make-up done at the salon. Only a few hours separated us from adding a new chapter to our family history. Soon we would eat *maqluba*, then go early to the celebration so we could get a table at the front of the room. An hour before the party's start, Safaa was in her graduation gown, waiting for us to arrive at the celebration hall. It was at that moment when, without warning, explosions shook Gaza City.

'It might just be a rough hour,' I said to myself, still at home, when I heard the noise. I tried to deny that it could be a new assault. But then a state of emergency was declared for the entire city. Of course, the party was cancelled. We never even left the house.

All the enthusiasm in my heart turned into fear of losing someone I loved. I felt it course throughout my body, even though this was not the first war in my twenty years of life. It was my fifth major attack. I should be used to this, but I was not.

Soon after the start of the assault, Safaa returned home and we watched the news. Already, people had been killed, including children. Homes were destroyed. It all happened in just a few minutes. Before I had even chosen my outfit.

Hours later, I found Safaa alone in her room. She was looking at pictures of her friends dressed for graduation. I went to her with a trembling hand over my heart. 'Aren't you my older sister who is supposed to take care of and comfort me? Read to me some verses of the Quran. For the first time in my life I am afraid.'

She put her hand on my shoulder and played some verses from the *Surah Taha* (a chapter of the Quran) on her phone. They told the story of Moses and his brother Aaron: '[Allah] said: "Fear not. Indeed, I am with you both; I hear and I see."' As I wiped away a tear, I felt this was God's message to us. I pressed my hand to my heart and said: 'We all belong to God and to Him we will return.'

I was shocked, however, by Safaa's reaction to what was happening. She didn't even cry. Surely she must be sorrowful about her stolen graduation. Instead, she wanted to go to the hospital to help the growing number of victims. I tried to hide my anxiety at the prospect of her going to the hospital. I also didn't want to know what she would see if she went. I didn't want to learn what was happening to my neighbours and friends – and what might happen to me at any moment.

I looked for anything that would help me escape from my intense fear. I searched through my books for a novel to read. I unexpectedly came across the graduation party invitation cards. I felt I might cry, but just then the sound of screaming jolted me to attention. I ran to the street, where I found people rushing to escape from an unexploded missile that had fallen on to our neighbour's house. I realised then that trying to escape from fear was not possible.

On the third day, after sixty hours of bombardment, half an hour before midnight, a ceasefire was announced. I stood looking at the darkened sky, filled with white dots that were not stars but army aircraft. I was confused about what I should think. Should I wonder how long it would take for my sad, shattered city to recover? Or should I think about my outfit for a rescheduled graduation celebration? Will there even be a new celebration? And if so, will it happen before any other sudden aggression? I asked myself these and so many other unanswerable questions before I fell asleep.

Aseel graduated from university in Gaza the month before the genocide by Israel began. Since then, she and her family have been forced to relocate twelve times.

Art for more than the eyes
by Ahmed Alsammak, mentored by Deena Damen

With passion in her eyes and even the way she grips her brush, Palestinian artist Timaa Hassan dips the thin bristles into deep maroon paint. She is finishing the last part of a sculpted painting of two fishermen taking the day's catch out of their net. Timaa is making this piece for her blind friends and followers. They are her inspiration.

Timaa graduated in 2021 with a degree in fine arts from Gaza's al-Aqsa University. While studying, she worked with many media, such as watercolours and charcoal. Later, she began creating relief sculptures. 'This is art made to be touched as well as seen,' she told me.

Timaa focused on this speciality after an emotional incident in 2020. A blind woman and her mother visited a gallery where Timaa was showing her work. When they stood in front of one of Timaa's paintings, the blind woman's mother put her daughter's hand on the canvas to help her 'visualise' it.

'That moment, I was over the moon, and it triggered an idea in my mind to create art for the blind,' said Timaa. 'I communicated with another blind woman and told her about my desire. She came to my home, and

I showed her my paintings and some small sculptures. She told me how happy she was, because I thought about what blind people could enjoy. Her words lifted me up.'

Since then, Timaa has frequently shown her blind friends her paintings to get their opinions. Last year, the Gaza-based Association of Visually Impaired Graduates invited Timaa to showcase her artwork for five blind women, who gave Timaa feedback and suggested improvements.

'They told me they deeply wished I would sculpt the sea and fishermen selling their catch,' she remembers. 'But they also wanted some scenes that are not common in the Gaza Strip, such as snowdrifts. I set out to fulfil their wishes.'

Timaa has shown her artwork in ten local galleries, as well as one in Bethlehem. However, she has been unable to exhibit internationally. 'What oppresses me is that it's so hard to send our art abroad, because of the Israeli restrictions. I also suffer from a lack of art materials.'

Nonetheless, Timaa hopes to make a difference beyond the borders of Gaza. In fact, she has exchanged ideas with a school director in Bahrain, who connected with her via Instagram to ask her opinion on how to develop an art curriculum for blind residents in that country.

Timaa believes that people who have disabilities have their own strengths. She said: 'We exist to help and serve each other. For example, I help my blind friend with my art, and she helps me develop my English.'

Mai Alkhaib, who also is blind, told me that 'Timaa has made every visible thing touchable. I can identify the figures in her paintings with my touch, which amazes her. My message to artists is to take people who are disabled into consideration when you make your art.'

Timaa considers it a big responsibility to create for a visually impaired audience. It requires paying attention to even the smallest of details. Timaa's works focus on a variety of themes, ranging from Palestinian traditional dress to *dabka* (a Palestinian dance) and the evening meal.

'Our heritage must be "renewed". Heritage does not mean it is only related to the past. We add things to our heritage every day,' said Timaa.

Several steps are involved in making a sculpted painting, including much trial and error. First, the basic image is drawn. Second, three-dimensional layers are created. Third, other materials may be added to enhance the tactile experience. For example, sand may be mixed into the paint. The final step is the colouring process.

Timaa relies on her art as a source of income; the average price for her paintings is almost £400. Thus far, she has sold ten paintings. Each painting takes an average of a month to complete.

Timaa's dream is to complete a master's degree in art. Currently, there are no postgraduate studies available in this field in the Gaza Strip. 'I hope to develop myself in this art and to participate in international galleries to cater to the blind all over the world.'

Ahmed travelled to Ireland to study for his MBA in September 2023, just one month before Israel launched its war on Gaza.

One day in Gazan life
by Israa Mohammed Jamal, mentored by Katherine Schneider

I was making pizza in the kitchen when the massive sound of a missile strike targeting nearby houses erupted. The dust from the explosion came through the window and struck sudden terror into our hearts and limbs. I turned off the oven and ran to put on a long dress and hijab, so I'd be ready to evacuate the house as fast as possible.

When my nephew Kinan saw the dust, he shouted: 'Shrapnel from the rockets!' He thought the dust was rocket shrapnel that tears people apart and kills them.

His oldest brother Iyad said: 'Are you crazy?! Shrapnel is something bigger, which is sharp and strong and could blow up the wall of the kitchen and kill many people and . . .'

Iyad's long explanation to Kinan terrified me and made me afraid to imagine what could happen. I asked Iyad to stop elaborating.

We waited until the air strike was over and the fighter jets were gone before my brothers went out to learn what happened. Fortunately, we didn't have to evacuate and could stay home.

Kinan laughed and said: 'Look! When a bombing

happens, the people here go out to see where the bombs hit – no one is afraid!'

However, my little niece started repeating the idea that the Israelis would soon target our house: 'Mama, let's escape; they will target us.' Alaa repeated this many times. Every time, we replied: 'No, they won't do that, *Inshallah*.'

But day and night, the drones never stopped. Fighter jets came and went without ceasing. We followed the news through a mobile application called Zello, which informed us of the areas being targeted. We stayed together, children included, in the same room, listening to the news.

My brother Anas decided to send his sons to their grandparents, thinking that staying with them would be better. I decided to stop following the news and left my brothers when they started talking about further escalations. If the missile strikes didn't kill us, our terror of being killed would. I distracted myself by making some desserts with my nephews – *mabrosha* and cakes.

The children liked helping me mix the ingredients in the bowl. While we worked, Iyad asked: 'Which is stronger in its destruction and killing: a rocket or a tank shell?' I said: 'I don't know.' Iyad responded: 'I think it is the rocket.'

He asked this question and answered it himself at least five more times that day. The repetition of that question upset me, so to distract him I said: 'Iyad! Please, tell me about the skills and hobbies you want to learn.'

His response accompanied the chatter of his brother Kinan, who was playing the online game PUBG: 'You want to kill me? I'll kill you . . . Hahaha. You are a crazy and stupid Israeli soldier.'

In the early morning, we received a call from my paternal cousin, who reported: 'Feryal [my cousin] is dead. She went to the pharmacy to get medicine for her mother, and Israeli fighter jets bombed the street.'

This news shocked us all. But Kinan merely said: 'May Allah bless her,' and walked into the other room. I was disturbed that he received the news as if someone's sudden death from an air strike is normal.

Before we started to prepare lunch, we asked my brothers what they would like to eat. 'It's not the time for cooking or tasting new cuisine; just make a sandwich or something like that,' Abdallah said.

'I know we may be targeted or killed at any time, so why not enjoy life and live every moment and say *al-Shahada* [a profession of faith in Allah] at the same time?' I laughed nervously, and they laughed too.

Kinan said: 'Make macaroni!'

While we were eating, the sound of the drones stopped, along with the fighter jets. Iyad asked in surprise: '*Baba*, have the Israelis ended the attack on us?'

'Not yet. Eat please and stop thinking about that now,' was his father's reply.

The children of the refugee camp were playing football. Kinan and Iyad heard them and went to join in. Abdallah saw his sons playing in a street full of rubbish.

'Why not collect the trash, then continue your playing?' he suggested.

The children laughed and helped each other clean the street. Kinan joined and cheerfully asked for a shovel. I said: 'Great! Take photos.' Then Iyad also came, smiling and asking for a broom.

After they finished, the boys took a shower and asked their father to go on a walk, inviting me too. 'Are you crazy?' I replied. 'The fighter jets could come any time and target the streets or the house!'

The children laughed and said: 'When they come, we will run away quickly and fly into the house.' Abdallah was in a good mood, happy with his sons' work. He gathered his children around him and took a selfie, which he posted on Facebook. Then he shouted: 'Let's go!'

Just minutes later they were back; the drones and fighter jets had appeared again. That night, the explosions hit closer and closer, and we heard the news that Israel wouldn't accept a ceasefire.

We gathered in one room to sleep, the room we thought would be the safest place. 'Let's sleep with our heads opposite the windows,' the children said.

But Abdallah answered: 'When the bombing starts, both the window and the wall could break, so either way, we may die. No need to change our positions.' We all laughed nervously. Then we started to come up with ways to escape from the house if needed, and listed what things we should take with us if our neighbourhood were targeted in the night.

'Iyad and Kinan,' Abdallah instructed. 'If you're outside, wait for me close to the clinic street. If I don't come, ask anyone to call me.'

'OK!' the children shouted, without fully comprehending the danger we faced.

I recited a few verses of the Quran, and the children repeated them with me. Then I said *al-Shahada* and somehow managed to sleep.

Israa continues to live in Gaza with her family. She had raised enough funds to escape into Egypt, but then the border closed. Now, they wait.

CHAPTER NINE
2023 (January–October)

The perennials
by Eman Alhaj Ali, mentored by Kevin Hadduck

Dreams and homes lie together beneath rubble,
dust muting the bright greens and blues of a dream and a
  child's sweater.
Blood is the colour of a soul-scar. Only the bombs bloom
  now,
red, orange and yellow poppies rising over the desolation.
Sirens and the sound of missiles wake us,
echoing through vacant streets, as if shouting for people.

Mothers and kids crouch or fall to their knees,
their hands and faces pale as the martyrs'.
Waiting through the silence ravages our hearts . . .
Two hours? Two minutes? Two seconds?
Cheerful moments are pages torn from a book.
Sorrow is one long chapter in every Gazan story.

Another bomb explodes. Shrapnel flies.
Another home collapses.
Another martyr leaves without farewell.
The artilleries fall silent,
but we exhaust our minds with counting:
Two hours? Two minutes? Two seconds?

WE ARE NOT NUMBERS

Today, a man walks in his friend's funeral.
Tomorrow is his own funeral.
Breezes come from the sea.
Gaza cannot breathe.
The Great Omari and St Porphyry rise above green parks.
Gaza cannot see.
In Gaza, we smell only the smoke of rockets, bombs
and the blood of martyrs.

Still, we hold to our defiant and desperate smiles.
We claim the land shuddering under our feet
and the sea with its waves of aching.

Who will pay for the twenty years we lost?
by Yousef Maher Dawas, mentored by Nick Appleyard

People hate awkward silences – the moment a conversation stalls and a gap fills the space uncomfortably. So naturally they do whatever they can to avoid them. However, this isn't the case in Gaza. We enjoy silence, because it means a break from gloom and destruction – at least until it is rudely broken by the sound of missiles again, which make our houses sway and our hearts contract with fear.

It is the first day of the *Eid al-Fitr* celebration, in May 2022, and I'm in the home I share with my parents, brothers and sister. It's early evening, and the sky is a dusty pink from the setting sun. The evening's stillness is broken by heavy bombing, shattering the silence and blinding me with flashes of bright light. I'm in shock. Another missile casts light on the walls, accompanied by a soundtrack of furious thunder. There is a delay as the noise of the explosion catches up with the light. I jump with fright and grit my teeth as it makes its impact.

That evening we were all in our bedrooms, but as the bombardment grew fiercer and more frequent, we came together for comfort in a communal room in the middle of the house. This provided a false sense of safety. Of course, we knew that we were not safe, but we'd rather die together than alone.

I ate some chocolate to help calm my anxiety, a childhood habit that has stayed with me. My mother got up to make some coffee to distract us. But I told her that I would do it instead because I wanted her to stay safe in the room with the others. The bombardment in my neighbourhood was intense and we knew a rocket could hit our home. I walked to the kitchen and hoped that, if it was our turn to be hit by a bomb, it would happen after I'd made coffee. As luck would have it, no bombs hit the house, so I was able to fill the coffee pot and bring it back to the others.

We did our best to distract ourselves from the terrifying situation by continuing with our Eid celebrations – playing music, eating chocolates and drinking coffee. That night, nobody slept until the Sun was in the sky.

In the morning, my father received a phone call. 'Good morning,' I heard my dad say. I thought it was a strange thing to say because it was not a good morning. Had he said it out of habit or perhaps because he was grateful that none of us had been killed that night?

'One moment and I'll be right there,' he added, and without a moment's hesitation he ran out of the house. I wanted to ask him what had happened, but he was too fast and was gone. The rest of my family remained in their bedrooms trying to get some rest.

My father is a brave man and he always looks out for us. I knew that when he goes out into danger he would always come back, no matter who was around the corner or what was flying overhead. He had previously been arrested and detained for defending his land with stones against the tanks and guns of our enemy. He grew up as a farmer on land that had been in our family for several generations, back to my great-grandfather nearly a century ago, in 1925.

After a few hours, he came back. I was relieved to see him walking into the house again. But something wasn't right. His body was hunched over and he walked like an old man. I could see tears in his eyes.

'Our trees in the fields have been turned to ash.' His words fell like stones from his mouth. An awkward silence gripped the house before he added: 'I planted those trees. I nurtured them and watered them with my own hands. Week by week. Month by month. Year by year. I saw those leaves and branches grow.' He took a heavy breath and continued in a lower tone while trying to hold back his tears. 'These trees were older than you, Yousef.'

I went to my room to escape from the shocking reality that our family's farmland, which had been passed down for generations, was destroyed. I opened my laptop and put on my headphones and defiantly played the loudest video game I could find. This helped block out the sound of my father's cries and the rocket fire.

Most Gazans have their own way of seeking sanctuary and shelter in their mind. My escape is to play video games. I knew that youngsters in countries across the world were playing the same game as me – but for fun, not to escape death. And I lingered with that thought for a while.

A few nights passed and the war was eventually paused. A ceasefire had been agreed upon and rockets no longer fell from the sky. But the destruction had left something dead within the hearts of my family – a significant part of our history had been destroyed. I knew that many other Gazans had suffered far more. The missiles killed many civilians, orphaning children and shattering families. Some people were buried under their own homes, while others were killed in the streets. Some were maimed and lost body parts, while many of us who were left behind had lost a piece of our soul.

I didn't want to see our now-barren farmland. The last time I was there I had sat beneath olive trees with my friends eating za'atar, bread and olive oil. We drank tea, roasted corn and picked fruit. I can still taste those flavours and smell the air.

But now, there was only dark grey sand and the scorched remains of trunks and branches from trees that used to bear the fruit of olives, oranges, clementines, loquat, guavas, lemons and pomegranates. I put my hands on my heart to catch the pieces from falling.

I tried to reassure my father by saying the land would recover and we could work with the support of the United Nations to replant the trees that we lost.

'Even if somebody helps us repair the damage and plant new trees, who will give me those years back that I spent nurturing them and supporting them to grow?' he snapped back at me. 'Who will pay for the twenty years we have lost?'

An awkward silence fell between us. 'Who are we without a past or history?' I asked myself.

Yousef, who was studying to be a psychoanalyst, was the first WANN writer to be killed in the genocide by Israel, on 14 October 2023. He was killed by an Israeli missile strike on his family's home in the northern town of Beit Lahia.

A lost sibling and a resurrection
by Eman Alhaj Ali, mentored by Kevin Hadduck

Until ten years ago, I lived with a constant feeling that something was missing. I withered with loneliness like a flower in a desert. In many ways, my childhood was idyllic. My mother and father encouraged me in every way to live, to give, to love and to persevere. And yet there was a cloud over my head. I wondered why I didn't have a sibling to share my experiences with. I asked myself: 'What if I had a sister to share this cup of milk with me?' I saw other children going to school while holding their siblings' hands and saying farewell together to their parents. But I had to make that journey alone. I wished I had a sister to play with, share my secrets with, and be with me through my ups and downs.

Finally, joy knocked on my door. One day, while I was in my room studying for exams, my mom came to sit with me. 'Do you want a sister to play with, Eman?' my mother asked. I looked at her; she knew how I felt. 'I am alone, and I will always be alone!' I said. But she responded: 'Better days are coming.' I blinked in surprise and asked her what she meant. She told me: 'Maybe after nine months, you will get the sibling you have longed for.' I did not believe her at first, but then I hugged her. I was ecstatic!

We went shopping often in the first three months of my mother's pregnancy. Every day I looked at the new clothes for the coming baby and waited eagerly to see him or her wearing those tiny garments. I ruminated constantly about the baby's name and pushed my mother to allow me to choose.

And then those joyful moments vanished, without warning, as my parents and I sat at the table having breakfast. While my father listened to the news, he heard that there was an Israeli attack on the Gaza Strip. My father told my mother we had to go to our grandma's house, because it was much safer than ours. We didn't know the heartbreak waiting for us there.

Two days later, as my mom was preparing to go to the clinic with my dad, the Israeli assault came to our doorstep. A massive bombardment hit a military site near our home. The horrifying sound of the bombs made us all cower and take cover. My mom fell heavily on to the bare floor, and then began bleeding profusely. When she fainted, I started crying. I knew this was a danger to the baby inside her womb.

As the shelling continued, my father drove my mother to get help, forced to race through the same area where bombs exploded and shrapnel flew. Of course, they feared being hit by an artillery shell or rocket, but they survived. But when they returned, they gave us the heartbreaking news that my sibling had not. The baby had died even before it entered this life.

The death of my unborn sibling shocked me, but I

refused to show emotion. Everyone in the Gaza Strip was living through similar excruciating experiences.

After two unbelievable months of attacks, they ended; but they remained in our minds and hearts. We returned home to rebuild our dreams together. I entered my bedroom, where I had filled a corner with toys for my new sibling. My mom, with tearful eyes, hugged me tightly and said: 'Don't cry, sweetie. Your father and I will always be with you!'

Shattered, I could not find the words to speak. For a long time, we lived as if nothing had happened. This is Gaza; this is how we rise from the ashes. My parents always tell me that a painful experience can be a blessing in disguise. And indeed, we grew closer together.

Later, new joys came to us. My mother went on to have four more children! I now live with my parents and four young siblings. 'You are their second mom,' my mother says with a laugh. Still, we remember that first one.

A Palestinian woman takes charge
by Lubna Abuhashem, mentored by Jesse Boylan

Every morning, Amani Shaat starts her day at 9 a.m. by shopping for all the ingredients she needs for the day. Then she heads to her little street kiosk to cook beef burgers for the customers who keep her busy until almost midnight.

Amani, twenty-five, is the first woman in Gaza to work in a street kiosk. After she started her business, named Salt3 Burger, in January 2023, she was soon noticed by journalists and curious customers.

'They were astonished to see a girl standing and cooking in a kiosk on the street. The number of burger patties I had prepared for two days finished after two hours,' she recalled happily.

Amani's route to her little kiosk overlooking the sea on al-Rasheed Street took a number of twists and turns. She started out working in a wedding dress shop, where the pay was poor. Four years ago, Amani and her husband travelled to Turkey, looking for better work.

First, Amani worked in several factories, but then she found work that was more fulfilling: waitressing and cooking in different restaurants that offered Western dishes. This is how she learned the recipe for beef burgers.

While she prepared a burger meal for a customer in Gaza, Amani told me: 'My life was stable enough in Turkey. I wasn't planning to come back to Gaza. But my mother is very sick, and I wanted to be with her. Her treatment will last for a long time, so I started to think of what I could do for a living while staying close to her.'

It was her dream to run her own fast-food business. She thought about starting up in a retail store in the university district, but there was a big problem: the rent was expensive, and she had no money at all. And most of her customers would be university students who don't have much money to spend.

The situation looked hopeless until one day, when she was walking on al-Rasheed Street, she spotted an abandoned kiosk. She managed to locate the owner, Mahmoud Almuhtadi, who was running another kiosk next door. 'I told him I want to rent this abandoned kiosk. He said he used it for storage,' recalled Amani. 'Then he said: "You are a girl. What would a girl do in a kiosk?" I told him the idea and he was impressed and said: "I will give you the kiosk and I will be your business partner."'

Not everyone in Amani's life believed in her and many people tried to discourage her from pursuing her fast-food dream. 'People surrounding me told me I would fail in this as I had failed in everything else. So I was worried that all my efforts would be in vain because I wouldn't be able to do it alone without support, especially since I didn't have enough capital.'

But Amani was determined to give it a try. She knew she had two things on her side: one, in Gaza, beef burgers are only offered in restaurants where they are relatively expensive; and two, she could prepare the burger patties herself, according to her own recipe.

Amani sells a burger without chips for seven shekels (£1.50) and a burger with chips for ten shekels (about £2).

Amani cannot contain her excitement about how successful her small business has become. 'I was stressed out when the first customer came on opening day,' she recalled with a smile. 'I work all day. I am exhausted. But when a customer tells me "It is delicious", I forget all the tiredness and I feel as if I am over the moon. I don't know what my next step is. I don't even have time to think about it. All that matters is that I am achieving what I have always dreamed of.'

Lubna, her parents and sister were able to leave Gaza for Egypt three months into the war. Three siblings and their families remain in Gaza. Fortunately, her father is a military officer with the Palestinian Fatah party, and thus receives a salary, making life easier for them.

Does creativity only come from misery?
by Dana Besaiso, mentored by Deirdre Claffey

They say misery makes great art. From John Keats's powerful poems about his struggle with illness and death, to Vincent Van Gogh, who channelled his battle with mental illness into his dramatic and intense paintings, those who suffer can use their emotions to create particularly powerful and meaningful art. Misery, in other words, is a muse. But what happens when the misery is gone?

For as long as I can remember, Palestinians' stories have been flavoured with sorrow. Even our most cherished memories are, in some way or another, tinged with misery – whether it's a girl preparing for her wedding, a young man migrating to secure a better future, or an old woman wearing the key to what used to be her home as a necklace. A thread woven through them all is the longing for freedom and home.

When my eldest sister, Rasha, graduated with her master's degree from the United Kingdom, my family and I couldn't be there to witness her achievement due to the travel restrictions on residents of the Gaza Strip. We could only share in her happiness through photos and videos. Yet, I still considered myself and my family lucky that at least one of us made it!

In the meantime, most of her international friends' families managed to attend because, for them, it was as easy as booking a ticket and boarding an aeroplane. We had only dreamed of seeing a plane much less fly in one.

Since I was born, life, and the stories I write, have been tainted with agony. I grew up witnessing destruction, murder and so many escalations that we are nicknamed *atfal horoob* (children of wars). We even joke that we graduated with a bachelor of war degree, since we survived four Israeli aggressions in addition to numerous attacks.

We are so used to moving on after these traumas that we have started believing it is the norm. We pack away our losses, sadness and grief and keep soldiering on with our lives. We go back to work or school with the heavy baggage of emotions on our backs. But the weight grows increasingly heavy.

The last Israeli attack was in May 2021. The eleven-day aggression snuffed out the lives of 232 Palestinian civilians, including 65 children. More than 1,900 people were injured, and 1,447 housing units in Gaza were demolished, leaving behind people who now had no shelter.

I considered myself one of the lucky ones. After all, I was alive. I struggled with survivor's guilt. *Why me?* I asked myself. *Why did I survive when many didn't?* The question haunted me for a while. The thought that *at least I made it out alive* made me oblivious to my reality, to how I had spent each night of the eleven saying my goodbyes to my family and friends because death felt so close.

And then, life went back to normal – or as normal as it can be.

Sad stories are etched in Palestinians' DNA. I grew up listening to the stories of our grandparents and how they were displaced from their homes during the Nakba of 1948 and 1967. I heard about the massacres that happened before I was born, such as the Deir Yassin massacre of 1948 and the massacre of Sabra and Shatila of 1982.

These anecdotes are not just part of our history, but an integral theme of our daily lives. We face the brutality of the occupation, whether it is the aggression on Gaza or the dispossession and ethnic cleansing of Palestinians in the West Bank and Jerusalem, such as in the Sheikh Jarrah and Silwan neighbourhoods.

I've become so used to these stories, I stopped seeing the bigger picture. The repeated tragedies that affect almost all Palestinians made me lose perspective. This life is not normal. It is not normal to have an entire family removed from the civil registry because they all died in an Israeli bombing. It is not normal to be denied your childhood because you were locked up in an Israeli prison since you were thirteen for a crime you didn't commit, like Ahmad Manasra. It is not normal to be traumatised by the sound of a shutting door because it reminds you of the sound of bombing. And it is not normal to lose your five-year-old son, such as Tamim Daoud, because his heart couldn't handle the sound of F-16s dropping bombs on his neighbours.

But I also fear losing the inspiration to write if, *Inshallah*, the Palestinian reality changes for the better. I derive my writing passion from the ongoing struggle to fight for my basic, fundamental human rights. If I leave Gaza one day and I no longer must struggle, will I have anything to say? Will I find the inspiration to write stories in which people are genuinely happy, without the need to add 'in spite of'? Will I ever write a story about a mother enjoying her son's wedding without noting that it happened despite the fact Israeli forces recently demolished their home before their eyes? And if I do, will people even read them? It seems that it's only when we suffer intensely that the world pays attention.

I can only hope that there will come a day when we, Palestinians, no longer ask these questions, because we are no longer miserable. *And* we are still practising our art.

Dana is now in Egypt, working to complete her bachelor's degree online. Then she hopes to get a scholarship to study international law in Europe. 'As a Gazan, it's obvious that international law is being ignored. But as a law student, I refuse to believe it is only ink on paper. I believe that someday, international law can be used to hold the perpetrators of this genocide accountable for their actions.'

Dreaming of Palestinian planes in the sky
by Shahd Safi, mentored by John Metson

The weather was slightly chilly, with a refreshing breeze carrying the delicate scent of lemon through the air. As I slowly opened my eyes, I realised it was morning, and I found myself in the place I had always longed to be – my grandparents' garden.

This enchanting space was adorned with olive, fig and guava trees. It was the fig tree that held a special place in my heart. I settled beside it, taking in the lush greenery that surrounded me. Clad in my cherished Palestinian thobe – a black dress embellished with an embroidered upside-down heart on the chest – I felt at peace. The fabric of this dress was incredibly soft against my skin.

I observed an aircraft soaring high above, gracefully gliding through the air, leaving behind a long white trail. Shortly after, another plane zoomed by at an astonishing speed, capturing my fascination. More planes followed, and I wondered in amazement at the unusual sight of these aircraft in our typically empty Gazan sky. Normally, our sky remains empty, only interrupted by the terrifying presence of Israeli planes accompanied by the deafening sounds of bombardment. However, these planes appeared serene and beautiful, causing me no alarm.

2023 (JANUARY–OCTOBER)

I called my parents, who reassured me, declaring that Palestine is finally free from war and the airport had been rebuilt. They promised that more planes would grace the sky without terror or bloodshed, as the nightmare of occupation had come to an end.

And then . . . I jolted awake. I had been dozing and day-dreaming. I was on a plane about to land in Egypt, and I was on my way back to Gaza. My dream of a free Palestine was still just that – a dream.

This was my first journey back home to Gaza. Six months previously I had travelled as a student to study in Spain and was now returning through Egypt, since Gaza's (and Palestine's) only airport had been destroyed by the Israelis in one of our wars. I was about to gain first-hand experience of the numerous challenges Palestinians face when travelling due to the restrictions imposed by the Israeli government.

Once in Egypt, I approached a policeman at the airport with a question. I wanted to know if there was any way for me to go directly to Gaza without paying for an Egyptian visa. My plan was to avoid spending any nights in Egypt. However, he informed me that there were no other options: I would have to pay for the visa to continue my journey to Gaza. This came at a cost of £20. I only had 170 euros (about £140) to my name.

Upon reaching the baggage claim area, I was dismayed to discover that my two large bags, one black and one grey, were missing. Desperate, I approached an airport employee, who informed me that all bags from passengers who had flown in from Spain via Royal Air Maroc were still in Morocco. Despite explaining that I needed to travel to Gaza that day, she told me that my bags would only arrive the following morning at 8 a.m. She presented me with two options: wait until tomorrow for my bags or return to Gaza and the authorities would send them separately . . . eventually.

Having heard the stories of other Palestinian travellers who had never received their lost bags in similar situations, I reluctantly chose the option I least desired. I was both emotionally and financially unprepared for a stay in Egypt.

As soon as I left the airport premises, I encountered an Egyptian driver, who I told about my predicament in the hope that he would assist me in finding an affordable hotel.

The driver in whom I naively confided demanded 350 Egyptian pounds (£5) from me for a mere fifteen-minute drive from the airport. I was taken aback by this exorbitant fee, as I knew it was significantly higher than what was fair. The return journey to Gaza would cost 400 Egyptian pounds (£6.30) and take twelve hours by car. However, given my exhausted, fearful and lonely state, I reluctantly handed over the requested amount. Then I rented a hotel room for 670 Egyptian pounds (£10), only to realise later that I had been overcharged due to being a foreigner, unaware of the local prices.

The following day, I woke up early and arranged for transportation back to the airport. However, what followed was a gruelling, four-hour ordeal of wandering through various airport buildings in search of my bags. Each time

I approached a police officer for directions, he would send me to the wrong location. Exhausted and disheartened, I eventually sat in a nearby chair, sobbing uncontrollably.

A sympathetic police officer approached me and enquired about my distress. Desperately, I explained everything that had transpired. He took down my personal information and checked my passport before assuring me that my bags would be returned within half an hour. Though I was sceptical at first, he proved true to his word. Half an hour later, a woman arrived with my bags, accompanied by the officer himself. It felt like meeting someone dear to my heart, as my bags contained cherished memories from Spain.

I was filled with the anticipation of returning home and seeing my beloved family. However, my excitement quickly turned to disappointment when the driver informed me that the border between Egypt and Gaza was closed on Thursdays and Fridays. Determined to find a solution, I contacted a friend who had previously travelled from Egypt to Gaza. She kindly provided me with advice on affordable hotels to stay in and the cost of transportation from the airport.

That night, I became severely ill. Exhausted and miserable, I cried profusely before mustering the courage to seek help from the receptionist. With a debilitating headache, a stomach ache and a sore throat, I explained my symptoms and gave him money to purchase medicine from a nearby pharmacy. Given the late hour and my fear, I couldn't go there myself.

The following morning, I realised that my funds were running dangerously low. Desperate for assistance, I contacted my mother through WhatsApp and asked her to send me some money. Thankfully, she promptly sent it, and it arrived in just fifteen minutes. Time seemed to drag as I tried to push aside my anxieties and explore some of Egypt's attractions, such as the Nile and el-Hussein Bazaar. Although these visits were enjoyable, they were overshadowed by my overall negative experience in Cairo.

On Saturday, I discovered that to avoid paying any additional taxes, I needed to complete certain documents. I was forced to spend another night in Egypt before finally being able to continue my journey home.

Finally, Sunday arrived. Near the airport, there is a gathering place called al-Sheratun, where Palestinians convene before returning home. At 11 p.m. I arrived. Three hours later, I boarded a microbus, which took us as far as al-Emadiyyeah. We had no choice but to sleep inside the microbus since there were no hotels nearby. When I disembarked in the morning, I was taken aback by the sight of numerous men sleeping on the ground. It turns out that while women were allowed to stay in the buses at night, the men were forced to stay outside. I visited a coffee shop to freshen up, use the restroom, and have some tea.

At 2.30 p.m. Egyptian policemen inspected our bags. The first bus underwent this process at 9 a.m.; ours was one of the last ones to be checked. Thus, it wasn't until 3 p.m. that we were able to proceed to al-Arish, where we had to spend another night. On Tuesday morning, I woke up at 6 a.m. and had a bar of chocolate and some juice for breakfast. Then I met other Palestinians who had travelled with me on the same microbus – two students, a married woman, a man in his thirties and an elderly lady. We were all strangers to each other. The driver then took us to a hall where our bags were once again inspected, and our passports taken away before we finally entered the hall on the Palestinian side. From there, I made my way home, where I hugged and kissed my mother.

As I sit here in Gaza writing this account of my journey, I ponder whether I will ever be able to travel again. My greatest dream is for Palestine to be free and for me to return to Qastina, my ancestral village in the land now called Israel. I long to visit my grandparents' home and garden. And I would love to see an airport in Palestine operated by Palestinians, where we are not subjected to humiliation.

I look at the sky from my window: I see sparkling stars. They could be planes someday!

Shahd evacuated to Egypt before the Gaza border closed in the summer of 2024. She is now studying on scholarship at Bard College in the United States. Her mother and three siblings also made it to Egypt; Shahd's father and other half-siblings remain in Gaza.

CHAPTER TEN
October 2023–Present

Echoes of Gaza, from afar
by Basma Almaza, mentored by Juliana Farha

On 7 October at 1 p.m. Malaysia time, which is five hours ahead of Palestine, I reached for my phone, eager to learn whether my friend Noor had successfully completed her final exam of the year.

I instantly saw that my WhatsApp feed was flooded with messages, each more shocking than the last, about Gazans fighting beyond the confines of Gaza, our blockaded homeland. Messages poured in, recounting a miraculous breakout from the prison in which I'd grown up. But very soon, the news became more alarming and sinister. People had been killed or taken hostage. The Israeli government vowed brutal revenge.

With shaking hands, I quickly dialled my mother. My heart pounded. 'What's happening? Are you safe?' Her responses emerged only as fractured sounds. The internet connection in Gaza had been severed.

I placed my hand over my heart; it felt as if it might burst out of my chest. I'd witnessed five previous attacks on Gaza from my birth in 2001 until I travelled to Malaysia in 2021, where I am now living, but this time I intuitively understood that something was different.

7 October didn't come out of nowhere. The world

seems to have forgotten that for sixteen years, 2 million Palestinians in Gaza have struggled under a brutal military siege. We have been cut off from the rest of the world and imprisoned within its borders. Severe shortages of life-saving medicine, food, electricity and clean water are routine and make life in Gaza unbearable. As a result, young people like me began making life-changing decisions. I resolved to pursue my bachelor's degree in Malaysia, a world away from my family and homeland.

In childhood, I learned about our history from my grandfather, Salim. I recall how my brothers and I used to sit in a circle by candlelight at night, listening to his stories. Our tragedy – the Nakba – began in May 1945, he told us, while he was harvesting his olive trees. Zionist terror gangs forced our families out of their homes, killing men, women and children, prompting others to flee. Those who stayed witnessed the foundations being laid for the discriminatory policies we see today. My grandfather urged us never to stop sharing these stories of Palestine.

Over the past two years, during lunch breaks at my university in Malaysia, where students from all over the world study, my classmates and I often engaged in discussions about everything from culture and religion to politics. These are precious opportunities to share my grandfather's stories and my own perspective on the Palestinian situation. In all these discussions, I passionately insist on our right to defend ourselves from repression and to challenge the occupation of our land. In particular, the term 'apartheid' – a crime against humanity – often features in these conversations, as it describes the framework that governs my people's daily lives. If my grandfather were still alive, I think he would be proud to hear me express these ideas.

On Monday morning, 9 October, I received devastating news. A fellow Gazan student in Malaysia, who had returned home to visit his family, had been killed. In my shock and grief, my brain flooded with memories of the centres for learning where I'd attended training and leadership courses, now surely reduced to rubble.

The following day at 3 a.m. in Gaza, my family received a grim command: 'Evacuate immediately!' Knowing what was to come, they left with nothing but their souls since no means of transportation was available. My mother, despite being disabled by osteoporosis, embarked on the journey on foot, every step an agonising ordeal. Yet their determination carried them to a makeshift shelter by morning.

I tried to contact them, choking on my words: 'I should be there with you, enduring this together.' My mother's voice quivered, hoarse from the toxic fumes that had engulfed the Gaza Strip: 'You're safe, my daughter. Promise me you won't stop telling the world about Palestine.' The connection dropped, and that was the last time I heard her voice.

Later that day, the news came that my home had turned to ashes. Unable to even blink, I stared at the news feed on my phone screen. I saw nineteen years of memories: every past birthday, late-night chats on my bedroom balcony, conversations with my mother, hot cups of tea, laughing with my three siblings, and tears of fright soaking my pillow during harrowing nights of bombardment. In less than a minute, my entire neighbourhood had been destroyed, taking with it all the joys and sorrows of my past.

As the hours marched on, entire families were obliterated by air strikes: the Sabat family in Beit Hanoun, the Abu Daqqa family in Khan Younis, the al-Daws family in Zaytoun, the Sha'ban family in Nasr, the Abu Rukab family in Zawayda.

On 12 October, after witnessing five days with no news of my family, I suddenly received a long WhatsApp message from my mother. With communication so unreliable, I have no idea when this message was written. Here is what she said:

I am a Palestinian mother who has lived through many wars in beloved Palestine. This war is different; it's the ugliest and the deadliest. The Israeli forces are targeting hospitals . . . and only Shifa remains. We don't know if it will be the next target. They've bombed mosques and universities, used phosphorus and deadly gases, and forced the evacuation of villages and cities to the south. UNRWA is setting up tents on the outskirts of Khan Younis for those fleeing the bombing. We don't know what will happen after everyone migrates to the south.

Gaza has become a city of ghosts, with the stench of death everywhere, piles of bloody rubble and dust, and endless wailing. We're hungry, thirsty and sick, since Israel is withholding medicine, cooking gas, bread, electricity and all the necessities of life. We can only say, 'There is no power or strength except through Allah,' thanking Him for keeping us alive. We're sleeping on the streets or in overcrowded schools meant for 1,000 but hosting over 7,000. We don't know what awaits us next.

Tears streamed down my cheeks. I whispered softly: 'Mama, please stay with us.' An urgent desire to embrace her overwhelmed me. I am here and safe today because of her.

There is tremendous support for Gaza in Malaysia, with electronic billboards on the streets offering prayers for Palestine and demonstrations demanding an end to the war and delivery of humanitarian aid. Still, even when I surrender to sleep at night, the gnawing sensation that I have betrayed my people persists. I've slept just a few hours since the assault began, and the face that looks back in the mirror is marked by dark circles under my eyes and a pale, yellowish complexion.

All I want now is to hear my mother's voice. But I am here in Malaysia doing the only thing I can: writing these thoughts and memories so they are never forgotten. Physically, I reside in Malaysia, but in my heart and soul, I am forever rooted in Gaza.

Basma first went to Malaysia to study business administration in March 2022. With the exception of her brother, who made it to Ireland, the rest of Basma's family is in northern Gaza, which Israel has targeted for 'cleansing'. They tried to leave, she says, but they are 'caged in from all sides'.

I've been displaced from two homes. Now I'm waiting for a third
by Maram Faraj, mentored by Pam Bailey

I held my little niece's hands and we ran, ordered to evacuate our building at midnight. Warplanes flew over our heads, children screamed, and the ground shook as if it was dancing. Our neighbour had received a call from an Israeli occupation officer, ordering him to evacuate his home along with the rest of the residents in the building, including us. Before fleeing, I took one long, last look at my room, remembering how I had just made it my own a couple of years ago.

On 17 April 2021, my other house, the one in which I was born, burned down. The boys had been playing with fireworks, and sparks blew through my window. More than 65 per cent of our space was burned, and my room was turned to ash. It took us a year and a half to rebuild our home. I never thought we'd lose it again, less than two years later!

We lingered in the street for an hour, unsure where to go and unable to fully leave our beloved home. The warplanes circled continuously over our heads, and I told the little kids to cover their ears. I wet my clothes, I was so afraid of dying. Everyone on the street looked at each other as if it would be the last time.

But the Sun rose, and the time ticked by, and nothing happened! 'I am going to my home. If they want to bomb me, at least I will be home,' my mom said. I begged her not to go, but she insisted. Finally, we gave in and escorted her back to our home and fell into a fitful sleep, praying we would all live to open our eyes again.

Just three hours later, we woke to the sound of heavy shelling. At the same time, all our phones (mine, my mother's, father's and brother's) received many recorded calls saying: 'Gaza residents, you all must evacuate your area as it is a zone for Hamas terrorists.' Everyone we know in the neighbourhood are civilians, so we initially thought it was just a threat meant to scare us. But my brother checked and everyone in our area had received the same notice. We were certain then that we had to evacuate immediately. It was terrifying!

We called my uncle's family and fortunately they welcomed us into their house. We gathered as much of our belongings as we could and called a car to pick us up. Meanwhile, the shelling and bombing continued intensely around us. When the car arrived, we called my uncle again and learned that my mother's five cousins had been killed when the home they shared – just three houses away from him – was bombed. We hesitated a little out of fear, but my uncle said: 'No, come! Then even if we die, we will die together, and none of us will grieve or mourn the other.' We all got into the car but had to wait for my father. As soon as we finally began to move, a house just ahead was bombed. If we hadn't been delayed those two minutes, we would have been among the *shahid* (martyrs)!

On the road, we continued to pray for a safe arrival. We were scared, crying and reading the Quran, until we reached my uncle's house. There, we found his whole family huddled on the ground floor, everyone babbling in fear. They shared the story of how they had attempted to help my mother's cousins, to no avail. They were now just pieces.

We spent the next few days worrying about what would come next. Were we going to be bombed? Would we be the next victims? And if so, would we be identified by our bodies, or from a few remains?

I tried desperately to get an internet signal so I could contact my friends and family who are abroad. When I finally got online, I saw a message on WhatsApp. 'Mahmoud Alnaouq was killed alongside his entire family by the Israeli occupation.' I felt as if I had been stabbed in my chest. I refreshed my screen about ten times to be sure I was reading it correctly. Mahmoud? Killed? No way! He had just returned from his dream trip to Malaysia! I called as many people as I could to make sure I wasn't hallucinating. Maybe I was delirious. But it was true.

Mahmoud had joined the growing list of victims of the terrorist state of israel. No, I didn't spell that wrong. Mahmoud taught me to spell israel with a lowercase 'i' because it is an illegal country.

Mahmoud Alnaouq was (!!) one of the most passionate, loving, likeable people I knew. I met him through We

Are Not Numbers, where we both volunteered at the time. We began as acquaintances and gradually became friends as we did more projects together, even though he was a bit timid with female co-workers. He was one year younger than me (twenty-five), but in many ways fifty years older. He taught me so much. I remember telling him that I was afraid I would never be able to pursue my dream of studying in the US or somewhere in Europe. He told me that if I kept thinking about failing to do so, my fears would become reality. But if I believe in something, it will come true.

Still, he shared my fears. One day, he confessed how depressed he'd be if he wasn't able to pursue his master's degree abroad like his older brother, Ahmed, did in the UK. He was desperate to leave the Gaza Strip after losing his mother to cancer and his oldest brother to the Israeli occupation forces in the 2014 war. I reminded him of his own advice, and we mapped out the steps he'd need to take. At the same time, he was hesitant. 'Maram, I can't leave my family. They are the only thing I have,' he'd say.

When he finally earned a scholarship to pursue his master's in Australia, he jumped for joy. And then . . . Israel killed both him and his dream.

Later that day, I was sitting on a couch in my uncle's living room, the 'safe' part of the house because it faced away from the Gaza border (just three kilometres away). I was reading a random book to distract myself from the sadness and fear. I dozed off a little, until I woke up to a whining sound and a stabbing pain in my back.

An Israeli air strike next door had shattered the window, scattering splinters of glass! My wound wasn't serious, but I couldn't stop thinking about the people who were now lying under the rubble.

The same night, I felt as if I had a hole in my heart. How would I die? Would I be in pain? Would I be trapped in rubble and caught on camera, part of this televised genocide of my nation? I read some verses of the Quran and fell asleep.

I was surprised to wake up to the sound of birds tweeting. I was still alive! I was still here! My phone rang.

'Finally, Maram, you answered! I tried to call you but every time the line dropped! Where are you? Are you safe? Do you know what happened?' a panicked voice said. She was from my neighbourhood. I assured her we were OK. But what did she mean by 'do you know what happened?'

'The neighbourhood h-h-has been bombed.'

I interrupted her. 'But are the towers still standing?' (We lived in twin buildings.)

'Yeah, they are, but—'

'Then it's OK; at least our towers are safe.'

'But, Maram . . . Your home was . . . was entirely destroyed. I'm sorr—' I abruptly hung up the phone and leaned against the wall.

My tears flowed, my heart felt like it was going to beat its way out of my chest. I ran to my mom, wailing. She held me to her chest. 'It's OK, my dear. It's OK.' I realised that she already knew. Everyone in my family knew.

But they hadn't told me. We had lost our beloved home a second time. It wasn't only a house. It was a shelter, a place to develop aspirations, a nurturer of hope!

I told myself that the loss of a home wasn't comparable to the loss of beloved people. But I was lying. To me, my home was like a beloved person! It is where I buried my disappointments and anger. It is where I became the woman I am now. I painted the walls pink and purple, and covered them with Marilyn Monroe posters. I piled my bed with teddy bears for comfort during my blue days.

I wish I had thought to take our photo albums when we fled, so we could remember what it looked like to be happy, or to be kids. It's like we are suffering from a loss of memory. It's too sad to remember.

We never had a chance to feel settled in my uncle's home. Israel bombed the entire square behind it (and four days later, his home), forcing us to leave once again and walk two hours to escape. While fleeing for our lives, we saw the remains of people, their blood covering the street. Homeless once again, we headed to my sister-in-law's, where we are sheltering until we must run once more.

We are all going to be killed by Israel. This is what I feel. I have lost four of my friends so far, along with my home and my homeland. We are out of food and water. Many days when we go to sleep, we are hungry. I have had to flee so many times I don't have clothes or the personal stuff women need! I must 'borrow' from my cousin to cover my body!

I'm angry, frustrated and afraid of adapting to the sight of my people being killed and displaced. I don't want to hear anyone preaching about humanity, values and peace any more. Humanity is being murdered.

I am not a number. I am a person with dreams and feelings. I dream of the day when I will become an English professor or a human rights activist.

Please remember me if I die. My name is Maram.

Maram was awarded a scholarship to study at a university in the United States, but was unable to leave before the border closed. Meanwhile, she has been forced to relocate seven times, fifty relatives have been killed and two are in Israeli jails.

I search for food and water all day, then we're told to flee; yet no place is safe
by Hamza Ibrahim, mentored by Jim Feldman

When I was growing up in Gaza, my mom used to say: 'The earth flourishes after a storm, and even the darkest night is followed by the dawn.' After 145 days of Israel's relentless attacks and siege on Gaza, I finally understand that this was my mother's way of being strong in the face of adversity. And now I will need to muster all my strength if my own family is to survive this seemingly endless war.

On Saturday 20 December 2023, we were without electricity as we had been for over two months. As night fell, my family lit candles and prepared for bed. My little brother cried and pleaded with our mom: 'I'm hungry. Is there something to eat?' After my mother gently reminded him that we can only eat once a day to make sure we have enough food for the next day, we laid down together in one room. This is how we sleep in every war. If a bomb or missile strikes our house, we want to die together. We don't want to be like my friend Ahmed Alnaouq, who lost his entire family and will be heartbroken for the rest of his life.

We went to bed early that night, as we do every night. As we lay in our beds, listening to the constant buzzing of Israeli drones, we hoped for the oblivion of sleep before the bombing escalated. By 1 a.m. we found relief.

Suddenly, we were awakened by what felt like a meteorite striking Nuseirat refugee camp, the overcrowded neighbourhood where we live. Three Israeli air strikes had hit a neighbour's house. Dust and smoke were everywhere. I could not breathe. My teeth chattered, and my hands trembled. I thought I was going to have a heart attack. I shouted: 'Am I in a nightmare? Mom?! Dad?!' I heard family members crying with fear in the darkness. I desperately looked for something to shine some light in the room. When I found my phone, I turned on the flashlight. Window glass was scattered on the floor; the door of our house had been blown off its hinges. The foul smell of rubble filled our lungs. The walls of the house were cracked.

Gripped by fear, we ran out of the house and into the street. We took nothing with us, not even our shoes. The street was filled with rubble and sewage that hurt our feet and made the road impassable. We were terrified. It was dark, and we could not see much of our surroundings. We made our way to the nearest UNRWA school to take refuge. There, we found thousands of other displaced people looking for shelter. There was no way I could call relatives for help. Telephone communications had been down for two months.

Three days later, when we returned to our neighbourhood, I was shocked. The damage caused by the Israeli missiles exceeded anything I had experienced in previous wars. Three houses next to ours had been destroyed. Miraculously, our home survived.

Al Jazeera reported that 'more than 20 have been killed, 30 have been injured, and others are still missing under the rubble'. My best friend, Mahmoud, along with his family and other relatives, were among the dead. They had moved south after Israel told them they would be safe there. Their deaths reinforced what I already knew: no place in Gaza is safe.

Before the 20 December attack on my neighbourhood, there was a beautiful garden next to our house. I would look at it every morning and feel a sense of hope and peace. The garden was destroyed in the attack, along with those feelings.

On 31 December, as the world prepared for New Year's Eve, the intense bombing continued in Gaza. On 1 January, I woke up at 6 a.m. to the insidious sound of an Israeli drone hovering overhead. Fear welled up inside and I wondered what the drone was doing here. Then I looked out my window. Instead of the garden, all I could see was a barren landscape of rubble, sewage and uprooted trees. It looked as if our neighbourhood had been hit by a hurricane. That morning, I ate my only meal of the day, red beans. They didn't smell or taste good, and there was not enough to satisfy my hunger.

My mother was heartbroken. Still, she knew what we had to do. 'We face two inevitable dangers,' she told the family. 'Either we stay inside our house and die of hunger, or we go out, risk death from Israeli bombs and snipers, and search for water and food even though we know we might not find any.' Since we had run out of water the day before, I grabbed two yellow tanks and went out to find some. After walking for an hour, I found a place that sold well water and got in line. Two hours later, I walked home with two full tanks. The water tasted a bit salty but was otherwise drinkable.

It is not any easier to find food. It feels like Israel is starving us to force Gazans to leave. It's called ethnic cleansing.

Bread is difficult to find since Israel has bombed most of the bakeries in Gaza. The bakeries that remain have no bread to sell since they have no fuel or flour. After an hour of searching for bread, I came up empty-handed. But I kept searching. We had no food left in our house. If I don't find bread or other food, my family would starve. Just as I was about to head home with nothing to show for my efforts, I saw a crowd gathered around a clay oven. A man was baking bread and selling it at five times the normal price. After waiting in line for three hours, I bought as much as I could afford – fifteen loaves. My family wouldn't starve today.

Charging phones is also a challenge. Most people in Gaza have no access to electricity. The Israeli siege prevents Gazans from obtaining fuel to run our electrical generators. Thankfully, some people have access to electricity from solar panels. That day, I spent what amounted to a dollar to charge my phone with solar energy. This might not sound like a lot of money to people in the West, but any money is difficult to come by in Gaza. Like most people here, I have not been able to earn any money since the war began. Before the war, I taught at a high school in North Gaza that Israel has since bombed and destroyed. My dreams, passion and students are gone.

Once, a We Are Not Numbers volunteer in the United States tried to send me money through Western Union. I never got it. The one still-functioning Western Union office is far from my house. To reach it I would have had to cycle an hour down a road targeted by Israeli snipers. Even if I survived the trip, I might have come away empty-handed because of the lack of currency. A friend tells me that every day many people are turned away after waiting all day in line.

When I finally arrived home after spending seven hours searching for food and water, I was greeted by a flurry of leaflets falling from the sky. The Israeli military wanted us to flee to Rafah. I ran into our house in shock. 'Where will we go? We don't know anyone in Rafah. Living in tents is terrible!' My mother took control of the situation. 'We have to flee as quickly as possible before we're all killed,' she said. 'Family is the most important thing.'

Before we left, I switched on the radio. Western leaders were defending Israel's right to 'defend' itself, while simultaneously denying that same right to the defenceless, blockaded population of Gaza. I smiled sadly at the irony as another explosion roared in the background.

Although Hamza received a scholarship to study journalism in the United States, the Gaza border with Egypt closed and he remains in Gaza. He has been forced to relocate ten times. 'Every day is a challenge. The threat of death is constant, and I am always hungry. Prices for what food can be found in Gaza are sky high.'

The sight of stars makes me dream
by Roaa Missmeh, mentored by Sarah Jacobus

When we fled our house in Khan Younis on 1 January 2024, we didn't know where we would go. Survival was the only thing on our minds. The day was so long I thought it would never end. My brain felt paralysed, and my movements were slow. But it did end. And we found ourselves in Rafah, in something you could barely call a tent.

I discovered a swing on the land where we made a sort of 'home'. Every day after *iftar* during Ramadan, I did the dishes with my sister and then sat in peace on the swing. Because it's out in the open, it's a great spot for stargazing, which I love. I've been stargazing since I was around five, since the time I first noticed the natural world around me.

On a normal day before the war, I finished my homework, grabbed my laptop and mobile phone, and headed to the roof of my house to gaze at the stars. I'd observe: *there's Mars, and today it's aligned with the Moon. The Moon and Venus are looking at each other.*

Now, I continue from the swing by the tent. One night, I left the tent to wash my face, as usual. My father was out by the swing, although I didn't notice him at first. I looked up at the stars. They were so bright! And despite the horror that had brought us to this place, I found beauty in these stars. Moments later, I realised my dad was staring at me, while I stared at the stars. He was smirking, like he usually does.

He said: 'Well, that's one dream achieved.'

It didn't take me long to figure out what he meant. I'd always told him that I wanted to go camping and stargaze from a tent. Obviously, I hadn't meant a situation like this. But it was funny that he remembered that.

I laughed and stared at the stars for a while longer. Then I washed my face and went back in the tent.

I slept well that night, even though the day had been one of the hardest. From that moment on, I started noticing little details that could brighten my day, no matter how small. Amid all that's going on here, I realised that I can still achieve dreams.

Vincent Van Gogh once said: 'I don't know anything for certain, but the sight of stars makes me dream.' And he was right.

Roaa received a scholarship to study in the United States, but has been unable to leave Gaza due to the border closure. Her family have been forced to relocate ten times. 'We must always be prepared to leave,' she says.

I'm determined to run towards the sun
by Reem Sleem, mentored by Mona Sheaves

I lie on my back and stare at the corner of the ceiling, deep in thought as I usually am before sleep. I am still searching to this day for a refuge that will contain and console me in my exile, away from my home. I have said goodbye to my land. I have said goodbye to my childhood, my house and my companions. I have said goodbye to my room, my books, my pictures, my life as I knew it.

I am bewildered by my new reality. My reality now is displacement to another country, without an identity that is valued or recognised, without a clear future. I escape by flipping through my mobile phone, reading a book, listening to music that takes me into a fantasy far from the facts, until I fall into a restless sleep. But no matter how much I try to escape, I receive a slap from life that reminds me of the situation I am in.

I remember the day I heard that my university, al-Azhar, had been bombed on 4 November. I was with my family having breakfast at our home in Deir al-Balah when we received the news from a neighbour. I felt so angry. They wanted to prevent us from getting an education, which is our only real tool of resistance. It reminded me of the words my mother had impressed on me since I was little: 'Education is your shield, Reem. It protects you and helps you build a better future.' Now, there is nothing left of al-Azhar University. No professors, no students, no classes, no lectures, no books, no seats, not even a library or cafeteria. All the buildings were wiped out. My university was destroyed, and my dreams with it.

I remember attending the graduation ceremony of my cousin, a month before the atrocities began. I was excited that I'd soon be like him, wearing a graduation gown, carrying a diploma and waving it in the air, and celebrating with my family, who would be so proud of my success.

I felt such magic when I first entered the doors of the university – I was amazed by the magnificent buildings, the trees and wooden benches in their shadow, the wide halls, the terraces, the immense library, and even the gym. I took a lot of photos at that time.

One time, I was in the cafeteria eating my favourite breakfast of falafel sandwich when a hungry kitten passed by me. Feeling sympathetic, I poured a little yogurt on the floor for her, which she eagerly licked up. From that moment on, I made it a habit to buy extra food to feed her, and she quickly became my friend. I often wonder about her. Is she like me? Displaced? I wonder if she's under the rubble or looking for me to feed her again. I recall the words of my university professor when he told us that he would teach us translation methods in the next lecture the following Sunday; I was excited about that. I didn't know then that it would be the last lecture I would attend.

My family and I were forced to abandon our home when our neighbourhood was bombed. We managed to get to Rafah, carrying only a small bag of food and some clothes, leaving all our belongings behind. And then we fled to Egypt. My first night at my relatives' home in Egypt brought a sense of relief. I was safe, away from the bombing and death. But there was also a deep sense of loss. I wasn't home, the place where I had grown up since childhood. I had never considered that one day, I might never be there again. Memories flooded my mind, one after another. Everyone I knew had been scattered – some had died, others emigrated, and some simply disappeared.

Sleep never came easily after we fled. I tossed and turned in bed, feeling anxious about my future. Questions crowded my thoughts. What will happen to me? How will I continue my education? Will I ever complete my degree?

My mother encouraged me to apply for an online degree. I searched the internet daily and followed the news. After several months, I received surprising news from my university. Even in these most horrific of circumstances, my professors found a way for us to continue our education through online lectures. Fortunately, the university administration understood our circumstances and was lenient in many ways, such as waiving fees and allowing unlimited time for our exams. I bought a small table, notebooks and pens, and I began attending online lectures through the university's website. I downloaded the textbooks in PDF format and studied on my phone. It is a different way of studying. I miss the experience of being physically in my university, meeting my friends, going to the library; all the small things that I had taken for granted before we became displaced.

But it's an opportunity that I have to seize. I have decided to chase my dreams and create the life I want for myself, no matter the cost. I'm determined to run towards the sun in search of light and leave the dark nights behind me.

Reem and her family managed to evacuate to Egypt, where she is struggling to complete her bachelor's degree online. Meanwhile, she hopes to return home.

I miss you, my brother
by Mahmoud Alyazji, mentored by Umi Sinha

Today, I ate ice cream. It's been a long time since I did. I know you're in a better place, but I wanted you here with me, at least in spirit. I wanted to buy you the chocolate flavour that you liked; it would be my treat.

When I return home from my exchange programme in the United States, I planned to bring you that Barcelona T-shirt you liked, and heavy winter gloves because your hands are always cold in the winter.

I'm trying to heal, my friend. I go for long runs. At the end of the road, I see you, standing tall. You don't seem happy, though. You're making that face you used to when complaining about unhappy times.

Why are you fading? I'm coming. I'm running faster. I can hear your *Jadah ya Hoda*! ('You're a strong and great person, Hoda.') You always told me this.

Before I sleep, I see your body under the rubble. It flashes into my mind and makes my heart sink. Then I pick up my phone and look at our photos. I look at you carrying a watermelon on the beach and smiling, in the hope it will wipe out the image of your body buried under the rubble. But my chest is tight. I am angry. I want to scream loudly – loud enough for the whole world to hear me. I want to pierce their ears. My scream would echo my pain and conjure a rainbow of blood.

Mohammed, did you die next to your mom? Your mom used to cook for us and insisted that we eat. Or in your dad's arms? The last time we had a barbecue together, he taught me how to do it professionally and called you to take a picture of me as a 'chef'.

Last week, I told my brother, Ahmed, about you. Ahmed mostly doesn't cry, but I heard him sniffling on the phone. My mom cried, too. She remembers that you loved her *mahashi*. My whole family loved you, even my cat, Babs. You were our brother.

You were that friend who was always one call away, ready to help. A month before I left Gaza, you and the two Khaleds came to my house every day. I told you jokingly to go home. 'I'm travelling, not dying.' But you insisted on coming, and we talked and joked while drinking tea and eating *bzr* (sunflower seeds).

When I video-called you online, you said: 'Hoda, it doesn't feel the same without you.' I said it was only a couple of months till I'd be back. I said we'd go for *shwarma* and eat *luqaimat*. I never thought I wouldn't see you again!

You made a special video before I left to tell me how much you would miss me. I'm looking at each image now, tears running down my cheeks, heart burning, hands shaking as I write these words. I miss you, my brother.

I never thought I'd lose you like this. I'll never forget

that you and your family were killed by an Israeli air strike while you sheltered under your grandfather's roof.

I'll miss you calling me for a walk just to talk and talk. I never thought twice before telling you anything, and I am sure you didn't either. I'll miss you in my classes. I remember the countless times we laughed, and nobody understood why but you and me. I'll miss you showing me your eloquent translations. You were so talented and hard working. I'll never forget your smile, dreams, voice, positivity, generosity and kindness. You and your family were my second family.

I love you so much, *habibi* Mohammed Zaher Hamo. I love you, and I'll remember you until the day I die.

Allah Yerhamo – may you rest in peace.

Mahmoud is pursuing a degree in English and cultural studies in the United States. His entire family remain in Gaza.

A mother's journey through war
by Orjwan Shurrab, mentored by Pam Bailey

As a border area, eastern Khan Younis is always dangerous during any escalation with Israel, so we were among the first residents to evacuate our homes — just three days into the war. The first house we fled to was that of my sister-in-law, also in Khan Younis, but further from the border. The explosions never stopped during our first night there. I put my kids to bed very early, since nights are always the worst.

To distract us all, I played recordings of the Quran on my phone, turning it up to the highest volume to make sure the kids wouldn't hear the bombs exploding around us. The next morning, however, we woke to an explosion that shook the house, broke the windows and opened the closed doors. We all ran to our children. I rushed to hug Orjwan (three) and Nizar (two). Ameera, my sister-in-law, and Abeer, her sister, did the same with their small children. My mother-in-law shouted that we should put on our hijabs quickly and go downstairs, since it's believed the ground floor is the safest place during assaults.

I sat down with Orjwan and Nizar balanced on my legs, trying to cheer them up by telling jokes. I told Orjwan there were some naughty people who were behaving badly and they should be punished. That satisfied her. Meanwhile, I asked Nizar what he wanted for breakfast.

After about an hour and a half, we went back to our apartment. I asked Mohammed, my husband, to think of another 'safe' place, so he suggested we all go to his aunt, who lived alone with her husband even further away from the border. We stayed with her for a week. Since that area of Gaza relies on Israeli sources for water, it was now scarce, both for drinking and cleaning.

With water available only every two days for a few hours, we stored it in pails, pots and even cups. Our household now included eight adults and five children, so you can imagine the amount of water we needed. It wasn't clean, so we boiled the water for the kids. Orjwan, the oldest of the children, noticed the difference in taste and refused to drink it for a day, until Mohammed promised to try to buy the water she loves. He kept his promise. Mohammed found someone selling bottled water and bought her one.

One day, I called Mohammed, who was out distributing food in the neighbourhood, to come and eat lunch. Suddenly, a heavy explosion shook the house and broke the windows. I shouted to my sisters-in-law to leave the house immediately. Ameera grabbed her two sons and their bags. Abeer did the same with her baby. We all ran, leaving with only a glance back, some of us still barefoot. On the street, all the people in the neighbourhood ran without direction. Every face I saw is still imprinted in my memory: the girl crying for her grandmother, dead in a house just targeted; a young woman who couldn't seem to keep going and sat on the street crying, holding the hands of her two sons; the men who ran to help women carry their bags and kids, warning them to be quick, since there would likely be more than one target in the area.

I ran too, making sure that my sisters-in-law and their children stayed with us. I smiled at my kids, assuring them that we were hurrying because we were going to a new, fun destination before it closed. That made Orjwan happy, and she wondered about the possibilities of such a place. Could it be the mall, or the playground? Suddenly I looked around and didn't see Mohammed. I started to turn back to the area where the explosion had occurred; the 'target' had been the building of one of his relatives. The grandmother inside was among his extended family, and he had likely stayed behind to make sure no one was left under the rubble.

My mother-in-law shouted at me to stay, but I refused and told her to continue with the children. I returned for Mohammed and found him. He wanted to say a funeral prayer and bury the older woman. I was afraid for him, but I couldn't say no. He told me to go with his mother and sisters to the nearest UNRWA school, the Malak Primary School for Girls. I went, and we told Orjwan we were visiting the school she would attend one day.

What seemed like thousands of people were sheltering in the school. Ameera, who was still nursing her seven-month-old baby, decided to return to her family home in Deir al-Balah. We had become very close and I hated to say goodbye. Who knew when I would see her again? We spent a month in that school, and I called her every time we could get a connection.

Meanwhile, my mother and two sisters, who lived in the northern part of Gaza, were forced by the Israeli army to evacuate. I secured a tent for them and set it up next to my own in the grounds of the school. We snuck back to my house for a few hours in the early morning to wash clothes, bathe the kids, etc.

Then, on 12 November, at 7 a.m., Mohammed got a phone call. 'Yes, what's wrong? . . . No! Tell me you're mistaken! No!' he groaned. It was Ameera's husband on the phone; she had been killed. Their house was targeted an hour ago. She was the only one injured, and by the time they got her to the hospital, she was dead.

The next few hours were a blur. I saw only shadows of people, coming and leaving, shouting and crying, hugging and patting. Mohammed went to Deir al-Balah with his father to bring Ameera's body to the graveyard in eastern Khan Younis. I was afraid to see her body. It was my first time to lose a beloved one.

At first, I refused to see her. But Mohammed said that I would regret it later. I should say goodbye. I thought she would be bloody, and that the injury would be obvious. I was surprised that she was still very beautiful. Her face looked as if it was shining. I kissed her and she was still warm, as if she was only asleep. I begged them not to take her, that she would wake up. But she was gone.

An hour later, the family of Ameera's husband came

with her two little sons. The oldest, Hamza, is just two and a half years old. He used to play with Orjwan. Seeing the blood still on his shirt, I quickly gave him a bath. He had been in the kitchen with his mother when she was killed. She had been preparing tea for his father and milk for him when an explosion broke the windows. Ameera fell to the ground. She shouted for her husband and when she heard he was alive, she asked him to take their sons. Then she blacked out.

I will always remember how Ameera and I dreamed together, talking about our kids and how we'd raise them. She was only twenty-six and had so many big plans. She was studying to apply for the government's nursing employment exam.

But life didn't give us time to mourn Ameera. That same afternoon, Mohammed's aunt's building was targeted. Eleven members of his family were killed.

With no choice, we went back to struggling to secure food, water and medicine. Fortunately, we were in better condition financially than most families. My father-in-law is an UNRWA teacher. My mother is an employee with the Palestinian Authority. Both have stable salaries that helped us purchase the necessities, although many items in Gaza are only available on the black market and very expensive.

When a temporary ceasefire was declared on 24 November, it was a huge relief. I was sure that it was the end of the war. We all thought that the negotiators would keep adding day after day until a permanent deal was hammered out. I never thought war would resume and be even worse. But it did and it was.

Mohammed awakened me one day to prepare to return to the UNRWA school, saying the ceasefire had ended. I thought he was joking. It was only a few minutes before I heard explosions again. I rushed to gather the kids' clothes, some toys and a few other things.

I was so sad to enter the school once again after seven days of ceasefire. I felt as if the whole world had let me down. Hadn't there been enough days to expose what was going on in Gaza? The slaughtering of my people and the damage to my country were obvious. How could the world let Israel resume?

This time, the rubbish, pollution and number of people crowded into the school seemed to have multiplied. Then, after just a week, the Israeli army warned us to evacuate Khan Younis and move to 'safe areas' in Rafah and al-Mawasi. In Rafah, only four areas were designated for us to stay in. Mohammed didn't want to leave. He had concluded that no place was safe. He was tired and depressed. But my father-in-law and mother insisted we couldn't stay, and Mohammed finally accepted it.

We reached an area in Rafah called Tal al-Sultan; it was bare land with nothing on it. Only a couple of other tents were there when we set up that cold and rainy night. It wasn't long before we heard explosions and saw red lights in the direction of Khan Younis.

Mohammed's cousins were still there, and one of

them sent a text message, saying he was under rubble and needed help. During the night Mohammed had lost fifteen relatives! (Fortunately, the cousin buried in rubble lived.)

The next day, many other families arrived and erected their tents around us. Within a few hours, there was almost no place to walk. Thousands of people came, escaping from Khan Younis. Most of them had lost their houses and beloved ones.

The struggle to find water, food, clothes, blankets and other things escalated. Mohammed and I carried 10–15 litres of water every night for use during the day. For drinkable water, though, we had to be alert to catch the man who sold it. Life was made even more difficult by the high price of vegetables and fruit, and the lack of flour, baby's milk and diapers. My sister resorted to using scraps of clothing for diapers for her baby boy. Meanwhile, I worked to shelter my kids without letting them know there was a genocide taking place. I never would have imagined in October that the war would still be raging in the spring.

Postscript: We recently saw a photo taken from the air of our neighbourhood in Khan Younis, and I didn't recognise it. Our home is destroyed. We lost everything. So, when we learned I was pregnant, we escaped into Egypt. I cannot imagine delivering a baby with no clean water, no anaesthesia and no place to live safely. However, our hearts are heavy. Our families are still there, and our country continues to bleed.

The flour massacre
by Ahmed Dader, mentored by John Metson

In the darkest days of the war on Gaza, people prayed for the arrival of aid trucks. Although attempts to get close to them were dangerous – Israeli soldiers often shot at the crowds – we were hungry and desperate. When my father and I ventured out for such a trip, our entire family anxiously awaited our return, not minding if we returned home empty-handed. I remember countless nights we went to bed with empty stomachs because we had nothing to eat.

I remember one trip most clearly. On Wednesday 29 February 2024, my father and I travelled to find food for the nineteen children in our house. Ramadan was knocking at the door, so we wanted some food to break our fast, even if it was only dates, clean water, beans and rice.

We had left home at 10 p.m. the previous evening, and I thought we would be the only ones out at that time. But we saw a huge number of people flooding into the streets. All were prepared to face the brutality of the Israeli soldiers for the sake of some sustenance.

Al-Rasheed Street, where the trucks usually arrived, is seven or eight kilometres away from our house, and we were quite tired by the time we arrived. The streets were full of people. The scene was reminiscent of an army of ants, all marching in one direction in search of food. While waiting for the aid trucks to arrive, we found a temporary refuge in a destroyed building out of sight of Israeli snipers and waited there for almost three hours. We were tired and could easily have fallen asleep, but we forced ourselves to stay awake.

Finally, at 4.20 a.m., the trucks arrived to a cacophony of cheers. Thousands of desperate souls rushed towards the aid vehicles. Despite the rush of people, I managed to secure a bag of flour and began to make my way home.

But then suddenly, out of nowhere, came a fusillade of bullets aimed at our heads and the upper parts of our bodies. Many people who were hit bled to death, since no medical crews or ambulances could reach them. It was like a battleground.

I saw bullets strike two or three people at once, felling them instantly. Even those who were only injured were at risk of being trampled by people fleeing the bullets and shrapnel. The biggest mistake I made was not to take my phone with me to document the massacre that took place in front of my eyes. I remember well a young man who was carrying a bag of flour. Suddenly, a tank advanced and crushed him, smashing both him and his bag of flour into the ground.

I will need years for the scenes of that night to fade in my memory; the blood of hungry Gazans flowed like a river in the streets. The death toll was almost 130, but many more died in the following days, and around 800 were injured, most of them seriously.

Amid the chaos and devastation, I ran desperately for survival. Luck was on my side. With my bag of flour, I managed to escape the carnage. As I hurried back, I forgot to wait for my dad at the spot he had designated. Overwhelmed by exhaustion and the joy of obtaining some precious flour, I made my way home, unaware of what had happened to him.

When I finally arrived, Mama rushed to me, embracing me tightly, with tears streaming down her face while I tried to console her. She remained frantic until my father arrived as well, calling out to ask if I had made it home. She replied with a relieved 'yes!' In that moment, a heavy burden lifted from her shoulders, and she thanked God for our safety. I later learned Dad had been terrified for me but couldn't wait any longer, assuming I had already returned. He started home, clutching a packet of dates in his hands, narrowly escaping being run over by an approaching truck.

I will always remember the young man with the bag of flour who was crushed by the tank. In my mind, he will forever have a place in history as a symbol of the courage of the Gazan people, standing firmly in their resistance to ethnic cleansing and their will to survive.

Ahmed is still in Gaza and has been forced to relocate more than nine times. At one point, his home was

destroyed, and his eight-month-old unborn daughter died when he and his wife were buried under rubble for three days. She would have been named Arya.

Love amid chaos
by Samah Abushaibah, mentored by Jim Feldman

In a world filled with pain, love has the power to transcend barriers and endure the harshest of circumstances. I learned this truth from my friend, Hind, and the love of her life, Malik, two souls bound by love, whose journey took an unexpected turn.

Malik first noticed Hind when they were neighbours in the Zaytoun neighbourhood near Gaza City. Hind immediately captured Malik's heart with her big eyes and hopeful smile. Soon after they met, Malik knew he wanted to marry Hind and sought her father's permission, as is traditional. The engagement may have been a traditional one, but the love Hind felt for Malik was real. She loved his loyalty, his sense of humour and his generosity.

Because of the challenges they faced, from poverty to the lack of work, they did not set a date for their wedding for two years. During this time, their bond continued to grow stronger. Whenever people asked why they had not married, they said they were not ready.

Hind often reminisced about the early days of their engagement, recalling Malik's gentleness and unwavering support. 'We both believe love is a promise of a warm house with kids messing around, and me cooking him his favourite dish and eating it together.'

7 October was the day Hind was supposed to pick up her dress and Malik was scheduled to check out the wedding hall. But instead, Hind's cousin was killed in an Israeli bombing raid. A wedding, even a small one, is now an impossible dream until the war ends.

Malik's focus immediately switched from his wedding day to saving lives. Because he is a paramedic, he saw it as his duty to go to Shifa Hospital in Gaza City in the north and help in any way he could. This left Hind with no choice but to travel with her family to her aunt's house in the middle of Gaza. Until then, Hind and Malik had always been neighbours. Now they were separated by miles and besieged by fear. Their only solace came two months into the war, when they were able to have occasional phone conversations.

Hind recounts the agonising wait between calls, her heart heavy with worry. 'I spend the time waiting for any news related to him.'

Two months into the war, tragedy struck. While Malik was caring for an injured civilian, shrapnel from an explosion pierced his abdomen, destroying half his liver and lodging in his back. Even after he sustained this grave injury, Malik continued to work to save lives. 'Whenever I tell him to rest, he says he can't. He feels compelled to rush to help others who have been hurt,' Hind says.

When his wounds became worse, the Israeli army refused to give him permission to travel south by ambulance, where he would have better access to healthy food and the surgery he needed to remove shrapnel from his back.

Hind's worst fears were realised on 16 March 2024, when Malik was taken captive by the Israeli army during its attack on Shifa Hospital. 'I talked to him a day before the attack. We laughed more than we had in months. Before hanging up, he promised to call back when the connection was better. As it turned out, the army surrounded the hospital faster than we thought it would and he couldn't call me.'

Hind fell into deep despair. The uncertainty of his fate weighed heavily on her. For the next twenty-five days, Hind and her family lived with uncertainty about Malik's fate. Then they saw a news report about Palestinians abducted by the Israeli army from Shifa Hospital. There, in a photograph of IDs taken from the abductees, was Malik's identification card.

Despite the overwhelming odds of being reunited with Malik any time soon, if ever, Hind clings to hope, refusing to let go of the love that sustains her. 'My Malik is fine. That's what my heart tells me.'

Samah remains in Gaza and has been forced to evacuate ten times. Three cousins have been killed and her fiancé is stuck in northern Gaza, unable to leave due to Israel's efforts to isolate and 'cleanse' the area. Meanwhile, she is trying to complete her university studies online, often walking twenty minutes for an internet connection.

Searching for my missing friend
by Alaa Mahdi Kudaih, mentored by Susan McDowell

In the month of December 2023, all my dreams were destroyed, at the same time that I lost my soulmate.

Shahad Hamdan Abu Lebdah, who I'd known since 2013, was just twenty-four years old. We were inseparable, attending the same school and class, spending most of our time with our close-knit group of friends. We used to talk for hours, telling jokes, thinking deeply, and reading books and having passionate discussions about them. Shahad graduated from university just two months before the war. She was artistic and a beacon of love, inspiration and passion.

The last time I spoke with Shahad was on 3 December. I was checking on her and her family, who were living in Khan Younis. They were desperate to survive! She asked me if I knew anyone who could help them escape Gaza.

Just a week after our conversation, Israel attacked their village (located in a so-called 'safe corridor') with tanks, drones and air strikes. I read that Israeli forces had surrounded their home, and then we lost all contact with them. What happened? We have no idea. Shahad, her father Hamdan, her mother Amneh, her sisters Reem,

Razan and Tasneem, and her brother Islam were all in the house. My heart aches with the unbearable uncertainty.

The only one who survived physically, although not mentally, from this unknown fate is Shahad's oldest sister, Hala, who is studying for a master's in the UK. Not knowing what happened to them is torture.

After Israel withdrew from the area at the end of January, I tried to get someone to visit their home, praying we might find information about Shahad and her family. One of my relatives who had been evacuated to a school nearby tried to visit, but it was too dangerous because of the drones still circling the area.

Then somebody brought a dead body to the school where my relative was staying, saying they found it at Shahad's house. I was sent a photograph of the covered body, which bore a note stating the family name. The note also said 'unidentified' because the body was decomposed, and that it was assumed to be female (because of the long hair that remained, I learned). When I received this news, I started shaking uncontrollably, as if heavy stones were crushing my chest. I began sweating heavily, lost focus, and was on the verge of fainting.

Two weeks later, they found two more decomposed bodies of females in the garden of the house – likely other members of the family. Her relatives and friends who visited the house told me that it was half destroyed and there were traces left by soldiers who had stormed the place. There was also evidence of execution on the body with the note, and the two others had had their hands tied. Hala tried to identify them, but they were too decomposed. However, she thinks that one of them is her mother because of her distinctive teeth.

In my mind, I imagine the scene of the invasion, with soldiers storming the house and executing those in it. I see how, after the withdrawal, the people of the area find bodies in the house, and try to determine the identities from the remaining hair, earrings, bracelets or phones lying next to them.

Is my friend one of them? Or are these her siblings? Where are the other family members? Were they all killed? Were any of them kidnapped? Was everyone executed? What my heart fears is that their bodies have been stolen by the occupation forces and buried anonymously.

Shahad knew how much I hate the colour grey, as she did. We always loved clarity. Every day, as the weight of unanswered questions settles on my heart, I am consumed by an unremitting guilt that gnaws at my soul. I imagine her in desperate need of help. That I cannot reach her, that I could not be there when it mattered most, haunts me deeply.

I scoured every possible corner, hoping for a miracle that never came. The countless hours spent canvassing hospitals, makeshift shelters, and the wreckage of bombed-out neighbourhoods were futile attempts against a tide of despair.

I still cry a lot and pray that she is still alive. I pray for her to visit me in my dreams; and in fact each time I urge God to let me see her, He does. She reassures me that she has travelled somewhere better and apologises for her absence. The last time she visited my dreams, she hugged me and slept in my arms like a baby – small, delicate and beautiful, as always.

Alaa, who earned her psychology degree in Turkey, now lives in exile in Belgium as a freelance photographer and writer. Her family remains trapped in Gaza, and she carries the weight of being safe while her loved ones face daily horrors. Through her writing, Alaa honours the memory of her martyred friends and family, ensuring their stories are not forgotten. 'If the war ends, I believe we can – and will have to – rebuild not just our homes, but our hearts. After so much suffering, the scars are beyond physical. The emotional wounds will last long after the violence stops.'

Where is our home?
by Wejdan Wajdy Abu Shammala, mentored by Laurie Tuller

After ten weeks of displacement, moving from place to place in search of safety, we suddenly learned that some people had returned to our neighbourhood in the southern Gaza Strip and inspected their homes after the occupation forces had withdrawn for a few days. Upon hearing the news, I turned to my father, my voice trembling with both fear and hope. 'I want to go home,' I pleaded, and then, almost whispering: 'We don't even know if our house is still standing; please, let's just go and see.'

Despite the danger, as the area was still unsafe since Israeli forces continued to bomb other parts of our city, I remained adamant. I begged my father relentlessly until he finally agreed, though he warned me: 'But we won't stay long.' I hastily dressed to go outside and prepared myself, my heart pounding with a mix of anxiety and determination.

Our journey, which should have taken thirty to forty-five minutes, stretched into an agonising two and a half hours as we struggled to find a means of transport to take us home. Eventually, given the scarcity of options, we ended up squeezing into a rickety old car that, besides the driver, already had more than five people crammed inside. The vehicle – and the road – were in such poor condition that every bump had us gripping each other.

Every moment was filled with a painfully intense longing as I imagined our house still standing, waiting for us. I shared my excitement with my father, trying to mask my underlying fear, reminiscing about the living room that had witnessed so many happy gatherings and joyful moments, the guest room where we warmly welcomed many loved ones. I thought of our kitchen, where my mother, siblings and I shared laughter and stories while she cooked. My mind wandered to our bedroom – my sanctuary shared with my sister, where our walls held our secrets; my bed that provided solace; and my desk, a testament to my achievements.

My desk was carefully arranged to reflect my life's journey. Among the neatly stacked books, there were titles that had guided me through both personal and academic challenges. There was a cork board displaying a calendar filled with notes and reminders, mapping out my hopes and plans. There were pens scattered everywhere – some emptied to the last drop of ink, each one a silent witness to countless hours spent scribbling ideas, drafting essays and pouring my thoughts on to paper. Next to them was a big stack of notebooks, each with a purpose, dedicated to different parts of my life – one for daily thoughts, another for creative ideas, and others filled with plans and sketches. Small frames on the desk held memories and motivational quotes. And there was the candle – a small yet significant presence, reminding me to breathe, to pause, to savour the journey I was on. It was a simple reminder that even in the darkest hours, there was always a glow guiding the way. It wasn't just a desk. It was a space where ambition met reality; it was a witness to a future yet to be written.

Sitting in the car, even as my mind wandered through the rooms of the house, a single question echoed in my mind: 'Is it possible that our house is still OK? Oh Allah, let it be safe,' I whispered repeatedly.

As we reached the city, I could already see from the outskirts the extent of the devastation. We arrived inside the city after an exhausting journey but were unable to find a car to take us to our neighbourhood, let alone close to our home. The Israeli occupation had destroyed the streets, and the fuel shortage meant that vehicles able to circulate were scarce.

So, we continued on foot for about forty-five minutes under the scorching sun, its rays beating down on us. Our journey became more and more painful, as we discovered up close the extent of the destruction. We kept exclaiming: 'Oh Allah, what is this? Why all this destruction? What did we do? What happened?' My father responded with a voice full of sorrow. 'It looks as if an earthquake hit the city.'

We finally reached our neighbourhood. As I walked towards our house, I felt my chest tighten; my heart raced and my breathing became difficult. I began to cry, pleading: 'Oh Allah, please, no. What is this?' None of the familiar neighbourhood landmarks were left. 'Where is our home?' Uncontrollably, I started running towards where our house used to be, desperate to see it.

Then I found it. Its façade was demolished, and the building next to it was levelled to the ground. There was no longer any door to our apartment building for me to enter, but I could get directly into our apartment, which is on the ground floor, as there was no longer any standing wall.

I begged my dad to tell me it wasn't our house, even though I knew it was. As I got closer, I saw our sofas in the street, burned in some places and broken in others, confirming it was indeed our home. But I still clung to the hope that this was just a nightmare. I wandered through the wrecked home, repeating to myself: 'No, this isn't our house. Our house is somewhere else.' The house had no recognisable features, nothing was in its place, and nothing appeared salvageable. I entered the guest room and found it in ruins and its walls shattered. 'Where is the purple sofa and the silver curtains?' I cried. I walked into the living room to find nothing left, the TV smashed, and books scattered on the floor.

When I entered the kitchen, I saw that everything was broken – the dishes, the glasses, the cupboards. Then I reached my bedroom, and I was in shock. 'Where is our wardrobe? Where are our beautiful things: my desk, my bed, and my sister's bed?'

At that moment, the phone rang. It was my mother.

'Oh, Wejdan, tell me. How is the house?'

I broke down, crying uncontrollably. 'This isn't our house. No, it can't be our house. Impossible!'

'Why are you crying?' she asked.

'There is nothing left in the house. Everything is destroyed, and nothing is recognisable.'

'Calm down,' she said. 'The most important thing is that you all are safe.'

And then, because there was nothing to be bought in the market, she added: 'Try to salvage anything from the kitchen because we don't have many kitchen supplies. Try to get clothes for your little sister and your little brother. Take as much as you can, but please don't be long. Hurry back – we don't want to worry about you.'

'OK, I'll try to get as much as I can,' I replied, and we ended the call since, as usual, the signal cut off.

My father walked around the house in deep sorrow, seeing his life's work destroyed. Then he said: 'The most important thing is that you all are safe,' meaning me and my siblings.

I started gathering a few belongings that could be salvaged for my family – clothes, though bullets had torn most of them, and kitchen utensils, though many were shattered. I finished gathering what I could, ready to forget about the rest. Then I saw the words the occupying soldiers had written on the walls of my home, filled with mockery for Palestinians. They will remain etched in my mind. I also will not forget the bullet holes that scarred every surface – the couches and other pieces of furniture, the clothes, the walls.

OCTOBER 2023—PRESENT

But as I walked away, my heart whispered: *Wait for us, dear home. We will return.*

Wejdan is in France, trying to complete her bachelor's degree. 'I am here alone, while my family remains trapped in Gaza,' she says.

My Black Friday
by Yusuf El-Mbayed, mentored by Jess Rucell

The night seemed to be calm, but unexpectedly, silence turned to unbearable sound. For the first time during the escalating genocide, the Israeli occupation forces had launched a ground invasion of my neighbourhood, Shujaiya. I remember the weather was hazy and cold. The heavy bombardment made it look like it was raining, but it wasn't! My family and I left our beds and took shelter on the floor, trying to find safety for our sleep.

On 3 December 2023, my whole family evacuated from my uncle's house, where we had been staying for the past two months. As daylight broke, we walked to the Western Educational Region, in the middle of Gaza. Again, we packed anything we could to safeguard our survival. My little brother Zakarya and I risked our lives by going first with a one-wheel pull cart piled with foodstuffs, water, furniture and hardware.

On the morning of Day 11 of our evacuation, I was an eyewitness to an Israeli war crime. Two boys and one girl, my neighbours, were murdered in a safe-haven shelter by a quadcopter. Yet the idea of evacuating the region didn't occur to us; we weren't thinking of what would come next!

Palestinians don't have underground shelters to save us from the deadly missiles dropping on our heads like raindrops; our only shelter was in the government's education complex. My father slept beside me so that we could wake up early together for the *Fajr* call to prayer. But that dawn we awoke before prayer, terrified by the sounds of military machines approaching. They shook our hearts, and fear permeated our bodies and souls. My father and I tried to calm the children and my sisters. We said: 'It's only a tactical movement; they are heading to another area.' We tried to think of a way out but sadly there was none.

Time passed slowly while tension and panic spread quickly. A new machine sound became discernible: it was the turbine of a bulldozer that had reached the school compound's entrance. I knew because I stood up to look out of a window. I saw three snipers on the roof of the Ministry of Agriculture, using the position to kill or detain anyone in sight. At that moment, it struck me why the Israeli forces had increased their bombing: they wanted to secure positions for their snipers. Shrapnel flew from nowhere, penetrating the walls and windows of the classroom. We tried to hide under the beds, stupidly thinking mattresses would save us from the powerful munitions of Israel and the United States.

By 6 a.m. the military sounds decreased, as if they were going somewhere else. I took another quick look and this time saw three troop carriers and five tanks. Soon we heard a voice broadcast from a quadcopter saying that everyone must leave the classrooms and assemble in Yarmouk Stadium, where the Israeli forces had set up a checkpoint. They ordered male youths and adults to come first. We didn't believe this was happening. But when I went to use the toilet, I saw the soldiers moving their military machines to the sports ground. It was then that the men decided to submit to this order so that our beloved families might stay safe. I asked my mother to hide my most important belongings, including cash and my phone. *Alhamdulillah*, by giving these to my mother I defied one of the Israeli soldiers' tactics, which is to take everything from us so that we wish we were dead and they have something to gloat about. Others did not have enough time to hide their things. I said my goodbye, bursting into tears, not knowing if I would end up detained, injured or martyred.

Tears streamed down my face as I walked towards the stadium. We came upon many heavily armed Israeli soldiers walking back and forth with the most advanced weapons in the world. They aimed their weapons at our heads, making it clear that if anyone dared to resist, we would be killed. Speaking in Hebrew, they pointed at us to hold our hands up. We did. Then a soldier spoke in broken English: 'Anyone English? If not, all dead meat!' I responded: 'I speak English very well.'

He replied: 'Tell them, take all clothes, not pants, off,' and asked me to carry the clothes to a dirty, wet area on the ground.

I said: 'There's a dry area right here. Can I place them there?'

In a rage, he shouted three times: 'Put them in dirt!' The soldier then commanded me to tell everyone to line up quickly, arms raised with IDs in hand. I did what he asked.

After five minutes standing in the commanded position, I was 'chosen' to come forward. I felt a sharp chest pain and a cold shiver running through my veins. With a shaking body, I walked towards the five Israeli soldiers, holding my ID in my raised hands. They yanked me by the neck and repeatedly smashed my head into a wall, shouting: 'You, Hamas! Hamas taught you English!'

I wept from the unbearable pain, saying: 'I'm not, *wallah*. I'm not. My father helped me to go to university to learn English.' They didn't let me go. They swore at me: 'You're motherfucker; you bitch, you deserve nothing but to die like bitch; you're awful, terrorist!'

I replied: 'I'm only a teacher, nothing more.' Then, a monster of a soldier grabbed my hair, slammed me against the wall, and crushed my face into the earth with his boot and rifle. He asked repeatedly for my personal information despite me holding my ID. Then: 'Do you know any terrorists?' I answered confidently: 'No.'

At some point, I admitted that I was from the Shujaiya neighbourhood, which has often been a target of Israeli forces. I was sucked into a tornado of kicks and punches by the tormentors, who used the butts and barrels of their guns. I was bleeding profusely all over my body!

The soldiers twisted my arms until they nearly broke. When I almost passed out, one soldier instructed the others: 'Stop. Leave him. He seems confused.'

I said: 'I don't know anything about what you are talking about.'

That was the wrong thing to say. He ordered them to spread my legs and bash my genitals. For ten minutes they used the heels of their boots to stomp on my private parts. They asked about some scars from third-degree burns on my lower body. (In 2008, as children, my cousins and I played with unexploded bombs that had dropped into the ground on my uncle's farm, and there was gasoline in the garage near where we were playing; the bomb exploded and I suffered burns from my stomach down to my toes.) After explaining, they battered my sensitive skin with their rifles and boots.

Finally, I was no longer the sole object of their attention. They put a group of us in a disgusting area where animals had deposited their waste and ordered me to stay in a squat position. The leader instructed another soldier to shoot me in the head if I stood up. I was forced to stay that way for thirty minutes. An hour later, they handcuffed all of us and brought us down a staircase to the head of intelligence, to assess whether we were Hamas fighters or involved in a Palestinian faction.

After a long time, a soldier instructed us to go, using a 'safe' route they had bulldozed, and to go to the southern zone. Another two soldiers near the entrance of the stadium gave me some clothing, food and water – after I insisted on this! I don't know what made those soldiers have a little mercy on me. I pleaded with one of them to let a heavy, elderly man evacuate with us. He assented, as if letting the elder man go was doing me a favour. We left the compound, but the route wasn't safe at all. With drones overhead, the snipers tortured us. Every step we took forward, we were targeted. They shot under our feet and above our heads while we ran. I took the elderly man to rest in a place far away from the snipers. Weeping, I walked on towards al-Saraya crossing. I was so sad because they still detained my father; they said he looked like Yahya Sinwar, a Hamas leader.

At the Abu Khadra crossing, as I looked back with the hope of seeing my father and taking him with me to al-Saraya crossing, a spiteful sniper shot me. The first bullet went in my elbow. The next two entered my buttocks near my spinal cord. Praise to the Almighty God, I was lucky: they weren't explosive bullets. If they had been, the sniper's intention would've been fulfilled and I would be a paralyzed amputee. But Allah did not want that. Bleeding, I kept running. Then, I got some help. Someone used a university graduation robe that had been abandoned on the ground to fashion into a tourniquet. He cut it up and stopped the bleeding in my arm.

Ten minutes later, I was lucky enough to hear that Shifa Hospital had resumed operation (this after being destroyed and controlled by the Israelis). I reached the hospital and was assisted by the greatest medical team ever. They cleaned, checked and bandaged my injuries. They reassured me I would not lose my arm, saying: 'Don't worry. You are so lucky to have the bullets in the meat.' I asked them if there were any fractures. There weren't!

It has been nine months since my Black Friday. The pain remains intolerable. We don't have painkillers. I don't know if the bullets are still inside me or not; I haven't had an X-ray. I have neurological problems but haven't seen a specialist. I am still desperately trying to survive this ongoing genocide, and now am documenting it for myself, my people and for you – with the hope that sharing my story will contribute to its end.

Yusuf has been forced to relocate more than fourteen times. 'Since we've been transported back to the Stone Age, my responsibilities have doubled; I am the only provider for my extended family – four families in one room!' His older brother Khalid remains in an Israeli jail, his father was incarcerated and tortured by the Israelis (and now lives with the family of one of Yusuf's sisters in Rafah) and his brother-in-law was killed by Israeli forces last year, leaving a child who suffers a multitude of problems after losing his leg above the knee. Because his medications and medical supplies are so costly, Yusuf is hoping to get the boy out of Gaza so he can get the care he needs. One of his sisters has been reduced to begging on the street.

A wedding and condolences
by Tala Herzallah, mentored by Margi Keys

For the first time in almost five months and, for a few hours, the house we had been living in since the invasion of Rafah was transformed into a wedding venue. There was a bride with her white dress and blushing cheeks; a groom with intense, loving eyes; mothers crying at the sight of their children finally growing up and moving forward after months of dread; and sisters and brothers holding flowers and candy, asking everyone to pray for the couple to have a happy life away from war, death and blood.

The place had no balloons, no wedding decorations, no colours of joy and no special lighting. Yet, suddenly, nature decided to play the role of a wedding planner, sending a swarm of birds into the middle of our circle, leaving everyone looking up at the sky with a smile and a prayer that the next chapters of life would be better. Birdsong was the background music.

The groom kissed his bride, but his tears betrayed his inner torment. His father, who he loved so much, and his older brother, who was supposed to get married before him, were missing. The groom longed for his brother's advice about marriage. He yearned to see his father's proud gaze.

Trying to regain self-control, he stepped back, avoiding eye contact. As we applauded, the *zaghrouta* (an ululation that women perform to express happiness) resounded loudly, proclaiming that not only must life go on, but that we are also willing to love and share one another's joys, even in the most difficult circumstances.

Later, as we were still celebrating, I laid on the ground, looked up at the stars, trying to rebuild my relationship with the sky. For months now, it had been the source of terror and anxiety.

Suddenly, the scream of a man pierced my reverie: 'Oh, Allah, grant us your mercy!' I recognised the voice. It was my dad. I tried to run, but my feet refused to obey my order. I forced myself to run towards the voices.

I found many people surrounding my dad, who had fallen to the ground, his phone still in his hand. I could hear only one sentence repeated over and over: 'May Allah have mercy on them.'

'Them? Who's them?' I cried.

'Your cousin ... There was a bomb and he was injured. Now he is in a coma. He lost his wife and three children,' Mum replied in tears, her body shaking.

I had already lost seven cousins. Would I lose another?

I sat on a chair and looked at the scene that had been so joyous not too long before. It was like I was looking at a different world. We were all crying once again, but for a different reason. There was love, but it was fraught with pain. And there was no birdsong.

People in the same finery and suits gathered once

again, this time to lament and offer solace. Congratulations were replaced with 'so sorry for your loss'. Hugs of affection were replaced with hugs of empathy. Kisses were replaced with tight hand-holding. Future plans were replaced with past memories. We all realised once again how fleeting our existence is.

I stopped thinking and crying. I was worn out. Later, we all collapsed. Before I closed my eyes, I looked at my family. They were all sleeping and none of us had even said 'good night'.

I closed my eyes and said farewell to the day.

Tala is living in the south of Gaza with her parents and brother. They have been forced to relocate seven times and are currently living in a tent. Tala was awarded a scholarship to study at a university in the United States, but has been unable to leave due to the border closure.

Gaza, my homeland, we will rebuild you one day
by Aya Zaqout, mentored by Jeff Abood

My name is Aya, and I am twenty-three years old. I have been an artist for ten years. I also graduated as a dentist from al-Azhar University in Gaza, in June 2023. I have long pursued both of my dreams.

I now have an extensive collection of my artwork, in the hope of opening my own gallery. I already have participated in many exhibitions, but my dream was to 'star' in a major solo show. Meanwhile, I spent five years studying dentistry, which also is a form of art. Enhancing someone's smile, and thus making a difference in their life, has been incredibly fulfilling for me.

However, the war on Gaza has drastically altered those plans.

On 7 October, just two months into my year-long, postgraduate dental training, the Israeli occupation forces forced me to evacuate my home in northern Gaza and flee on foot to the south. Along the way, we were forced to pass through many army checkpoints. Israeli soldiers stood in a line along the path we walked, calling out names on microphones. They forced us to raise a white flag and show our IDs. They randomly selected young men and ordered them to strip off their clothes. I saw burned bodies strewn in the middle of the street. I will never forget that traumatic experience.

I left behind all my paintings, along with the tools and supplies I need to create art. I also have had to halt my dental training, putting my entire career on hold. My university, the hospitals and the clinics where I trained are all destroyed. There is no life left to return to.

My family and I were displaced two more times since then. Despite claims by the Israeli army that southern Gaza was a safe area, this was not true. Basic necessities were nearly impossible to find. Clean water was scarce, and aid from other countries was blocked by the Israeli army at the Rafah crossing, preventing it from reaching the general public.

But the most painful reality for me was that it was the longest period I had ever gone without drawing. I desperately needed to create, but I could not find art supplies. All I had at hand was a pen and some white paper. I urgently needed to draw to relieve my stress, so I settled for those. To my surprise, the resulting drawing is the most beautiful art I had ever created! But it is also the most painful.

It is a drawing of a woman's face peering through a hole in the shape of Palestine, as if ripped in the paper, her eyes lifted to the heavens in agonised prayer. The woman is me. I titled it *Searching for Home* because, at that moment, what I yearned for most was home. And finding it felt like the most difficult, if not impossible, task.

In April 2024, I talked with my family about the

possibility of leaving Gaza to resume what the war had forced me to pause. My family have always been my biggest supporters. They love my artwork and eagerly await each new creation. They were also thrilled about my graduation from the Faculty of Dentistry and looked forward to being my patients. Thus, they wholeheartedly supported my decision to leave Gaza to complete my dental training and continue my artistic pursuits, believing I could then fulfil my dream of bringing smiles to others.

You might wonder why we couldn't all leave together. Leaving the Gaza Strip costs around £3,800 per person (to pay the 'co-ordination fee' required by the Egyptians to cross the border). To save my family of eight, the total would be £30,000. This is an unachievable amount given the circumstances of the war and the halt in economic activity. Leaving my family behind was the hardest decision I've ever faced.

So, I travelled to Egypt to save myself, while leaving my family behind in Gaza amid the ongoing war. I didn't fully grasp the implications of this decision until I actually left, and my thoughts have been conflicted ever since. I am considered a survivor, but what does survival mean if I am not with my family? What is the value of surviving if it means leaving them behind? Should anyone have to make that kind of sacrifice? It seems that to learn and build a future, a Palestinian must give up a great deal.

Every day, I wake up feeling guilty. Was my decision

the right one? When will the war end? Do I have the right to live a decent life while my family in Gaza endures such hardship? A Palestinian begins to question whether they have the right to a normal, 'human' life.

Nevertheless, I hold on to the hope that I can eventually bring my family here to join me. I've enrolled in a university and started to rebuild an artistic life. My painting, *Searching for Home*, travelled with me. Today marks three months in Cairo for me. I feel guilty and helpless every day. My communication with my family is very limited due to their weak internet connection. The lack of constant connection with them is difficult to bear. However, I remind myself that I travelled for their sake. My future is intertwined with theirs. I hope I can someday repay them for all they've done. Despite losing the paintings I spent ten years creating, I remain committed to my dream of opening my own gallery. I believe I still have a lifetime ahead of me to achieve my goals, and I will make it happen. This is the nature of the Palestinian people. We are accustomed to losing, but also to surviving.

Gaza, my homeland: it breaks my heart to see you in this state. You have always been the warm embrace that nurtured us, no matter the adversity. We love you in all your conditions – whether in peace or in war. We are committed to rebuilding you into a loving home once again. You deserve our loyalty, and we will remain steadfast. Your freedom is near, so do not fear.

Aya is now in Egypt and is exhibiting her art at galleries abroad. Her family remain in Gaza but have not yet been able to return to the north. When they finally do, they know that there is really no home to return to. Their house, like so many others, no longer exists. Her goal now is to reunite with her family in Cairo. But to bring them out of Gaza once the border opens, she needs a minimum of $10,000.

Tell Them
by Huda Skaik, mentored by Christa Bruhn

Tell them,
Tell them,
we are more than numbers,
more than silent echoes
in a ledger of loss,
we are families
entwined in love,
friends,
living in the shadows
of our hopes,
bound by dreams.

Tell them,
Dr Refaat Alareer's words
still ring
in our hearts,
his voice whispers
in foreign streets,
in every glance
we cast at the sky,
where the kite
of his spirit soars,

we tread his path,
weaving stories
from his legacy.
Tell them,
Zina calls for her father,
Ismael Alghoul,
with a voice
hushed by grief,
snatched away
by Zionist forces
that deemed
his journalistic truth
a threat,
alongside his cameraman,
Rami Alrifi,
who shared his fate.

Tell them,
not only Zina weeps
for her lost father,
but also Dania,
Roshdi Sarraj's daughter,
whose life was
cruelly cut short
by those same Zionist forces.
Such beautiful, innocent souls,
like Zina and Dania,
will grow up

without their heroes,
without their fathers.

Tell them,
the courageous Hind Khoudary,
and countless others like her,
march on,
carrying the torch
of Ismael, Roshdi and Rami.

Tell them,
Ali Jadallah, though shattered,
continues to capture our agony
through his camera
with unyielding strength.

Tell them,
Mohammed Zaher Hamo,
my colleague,
lost his life and family,
a young soul cut down,
his pen and heart
stilled too early.

Tell them,
our people are torn apart,
women and children
bearing the brunt
of relentless cruelty.

Tell them,
the skies above Gaza
are ours no more,
occupied
by drones,
bombs
and gunships,
each bullet
a symbol of their wrath.

Tell them,
in Gaza, fathers bury sons,
children's cries
pierce the night
for lost parents.

Tell them,
our martyrs
– more than 40,000 –
lie beneath the earth,
each a story untold,
a life cut short,
a family left bereft,
their spirits light our path,
urging us forward.

Tell them,
we shall avenge them
with our voices,

with ink and pen,
with memory and prayer.

Tell them,
they will forever
reside in our hearts.
But tell me,
how can we live,
the living
endure,
without
our beloved ones?

Huda is still 'telling the world' from Gaza. She has been forced to relocate eleven times, and is struggling to complete her bachelor's degree online, disrupted by the constant evacuations, unstable internet and unending stress.

Epilogue
Reflections from the founders
Ahmed Alnaouq and Pam Bailey

We Are Not Numbers is a project born from war.

War is what brought the two of us together and what inspired an initiative that has grown larger and more influential than we thought possible back in 2014.

In 2024, it is once again war – far more brutal than we could have ever envisioned – that has brought us to a defining moment in the project's history. In a way, the We Are Not Numbers story reflects the story of the Palestinians writ large: our progress is divided by periods of violence, with awareness of our work spiking each time bloodshed forces world attention back.

In 2022, after eight years of nurturing We Are Not Numbers into adulthood, I (Pam) passed the reins of leadership to Ahmed, a fitting evolution for this Palestinian-focused initiative. I stepped away to create another non-profit organisation in the United States, launching a similar storytelling initiative to give voice to another oft-misunderstood population: people in prison, often for decades.

Ahmed assumed leadership of WANN, internationally, full-time.

EPILOGUE

Over time, the two of us began to drift apart.

And then came 7 October. The shock of the brutality unleashed on that day brought us back together, reminding us that a relationship forged in fire, shaped by mutual respect and fed by a mutual desire to effect change in the world can't just be put aside. We reunited in the shared labour of love that is We Are Not Numbers.

In that first month, on 22 October 2023, an Israeli bombardment killed twenty-one of Ahmed's family members: his father, three of his sisters, his two brothers, fourteen nephews and nieces, and a cousin.

Although the name of our project proclaims that Palestinian lives '*are not numbers*', it was the sheer number of his relatives struck at one time that attracted a flood of media attention to both Ahmed and the project. Foreign media are barred from on-the-ground reporting in Gaza, and they were hungry for new story angles. Since his family members were slaughtered in their sleep, Ahmed's social media following on X (formerly called Twitter) soared to over 90,000. And the attention to We Are Not Numbers followed suit, with visits to the website accelerating more than 340 per cent. Meanwhile, he has been invited to speak both online and in person around Europe and elsewhere. More people know about We Are Not Numbers today than we had ever hoped – even winning a Front Line Defenders Award for Human Rights Defenders at Risk.

And the resulting publicity also brought us Jessica Craig, the agent who helped make this book – long our dream – a reality.

But ... why not earlier? Our young storytellers have literally written their hearts out every year since 2015, sharing the persistent lack of life-saving medical care, dearth of ways to earn income, undrinkable water, seemingly endless electricity outages, etc., etc., etc. Yet, except for a relatively small network of activists around the world, no one paid sustained attention, and their grinding existence churned on.

We are inevitably asked if we condemn the 7 October attack on Israel. Let us be clear: WANN is rooted in principles of non-violence. Our writers show the world in their stories that they are a generation whose lives have been shaped by Israeli assaults, occupation and blockade. 7 October must be seen in the context of the years leading up to that day. The lesson the world seemed intent on teaching is that it's only through violence – either done to them or by resistance – that Palestinians attract sustained attention on the world stage. Non-violent protests (like the Great Return March of 2018–2019), petitions to the UN, filings with the International Criminal Court – these steps have all been tried and ignored or quickly forgotten.

That lesson is being taught again with this war. Eleven months in, as we write this, the plight of the Palestinian people is a top concern even in the presidential election in the United States, which has been Israel's greatest supporter. In July 2024, a Gallup poll found that more Americans opposed the Israeli military action in Gaza (48 per cent) than supported it (42 per cent). Today,

EPILOGUE

when Pam talks about We Are Not Numbers to non-activist acquaintances, like her dentist or a store cashier, she is met with sympathy, rather than with a frown or total ignorance, as she observed in 2015.

Unfortunately, however, that shift has not translated into government action. Lobbyist dollars count more than public sentiment. Thus, the war continues. The word that best describes Israel's intentions is 'annihilation'.

We cannot predict Gaza's near future. *Will fighting between the two sides continue off and on, ceasefire or not? Will Israel impose a military government to rule Gaza? Will the so-called international community fund a full reconstruction of Gaza and insist that Israel allow the necessary supplies and manpower in? How long will that take? Will an entire generation of Palestinians in Gaza be 'lost' to trauma and a lack of education?*

We don't know. It's frightening to contemplate. But we know this: resistance to the occupation will continue, even if it is forced. The will for self-determination and a decent life for one's family cannot be permanently snuffed out. It's a lesson Israel refuses to learn, even as its own people want the same.

We Are Not Numbers will also continue to expand, although many of our writers are now in exile and we must change the way we have traditionally operated for the foreseeable future: in-person training workshops and *tashas* (get-togethers on the beach) are no longer practical, so we find each other and recruit new voices via WhatsApp. Resources will be needed in the future to translate our stories from Arabic to English, since language instruction is inevitably suffering due to basic concerns about survival and the destruction of schools and universities.

Meanwhile, given the increased numbers of Palestinians fleeing their homeland, new chapters of WANN are already springing up where our exiles find themselves – from Egypt to Turkey to the United Kingdom to America. If we publish a second book for the twentieth anniversary of the founding of We Are Not Numbers, it will be more of a mosaic in terms of writer location.

But the We Are Not Numbers contingent in Gaza will remain our beating heart. And thus, we end this book how it began, with Refaat's now immortal words:

> *If I must die,*
> *you must live*
> *to tell my story.*
> *Let it bring hope,*
> *let it be a tale.*

Acknowledgements

In addition to the individuals who supported Pam when she first came up with her 'crazy idea' for We Are Not Numbers in 2014 – mentioned in the introduction to this book – many others have helped Pam and Ahmed grow WANN over the years.

First, we cannot come close to expressing our full appreciation for the 385 Palestinian young adults who joined the WANN team of contributors over the years. Without their willingness to share their personal stories with the world, despite the adverse conditions under which so many of them must live, this book would never have come to be. Our only regret is that we could not include more of their heartfelt essays and poems in this first volume.

That brings us to the 162 mentors – professional writers, authors, teachers and communicators – around the world who have volunteered their time to coach our budding writers on their English and writing skills. In many cases, they became personal friends, champions and (especially during the wars) fundraisers for their mentees. Again, only a few of these individuals could be acknowledged in this book.

Two of the individuals who began as mentors now work in a much larger capacity for We Are Not Numbers, again as volunteers: Catherine Baker, who serves as our senior editor and website manager, and Alice Rothchild, who coordinates our mentor network. To them, we extend a very special thanks.

Then there is Jessica Craig, of Craig Literary. This book had only been a dream until Jessica found us. Without her it would not have become a reality, and we would not have linked with Penguin Random House UK, whose team showed a passion and urgency for our project that accelerated its development so it could come out when it was most needed.

It takes a village, as they say, and we are so fortunate to have found such a supportive one.

Ahmed Alnaouq and Pam Bailey
December 2024